THE LAUGHTER FACTOR

THE LAUGHTER FACTOR

Dan Keller

Copyright © 2000 by Daniel L. Keller.

Library of Congress Number:		99-91951
ISBN #:	Hardcover	0-7388-1432-6
	Softcover	0-7388-1433-4

All rights reserved. No part of this book may be reproduced or transmitted in any form or by any means, electronic or mechanical, including photocopying, recording, or by any information storage and retrieval system, without permission in writing from the copyright owner.

This is not a work of fiction. Patients' names have been changed to protect anonymity.

This book was printed in the United States of America.

To order additional copies of this book, contact:
Xlibris Corporation
1-888-7-XLIBRIS
www.Xlibris.com
Orders@Xlibris.com

CONTENTS

ACKNOWLEDGEMENTS 9
PROLOGUE TO THE LAUGHTER FACTOR 11

CHAPTER I
    GO AHEAD AND LAUGH 15
CHAPTER II
    WELCOME TO THE FUNNY FARM 22
CHAPTER III
    THE ANATOMY OF A CHORTLE 34
CHAPTER IV
    TRICKS OF THE TRADE 42
CHAPTER V
    THE JOKE'S ON ME 54
CHAPTER VI
    THE LAST DUCK TO GIGGLE 70
CHAPTER VII
    YOU'RE KILLING ME 85
CHAPTER VIII
    THE CONTORTIONS OF A GUFFAW 97
CHAPTER IX
    DID FREUD SNICKER? 106
CHAPTER X
    I COULD HAVE DIED LAUGHING 121
CHAPTER XI
    CHUCKLED ABSTRACTIONS 131
CHAPTER XII
    EASY FOR YOU TO LAUGH 151
CHAPTER XIII
    APPENDIX AND LIVER 162

ENDNOTES 167
EPILOGUE 173

IN MEMORY OF JAN HOWARD, A TRUE FRIEND,
WHOSE MERRY SPIRIT TOUCHED SO MANY.

ACKNOWLEDGEMENTS

I thank that motley band of humor mongers from The Institute for the Advancement of Human Behavior. Their conventions on "The Power of Laughter and Play" (via the half-serious profundity of Joel Goodman, Norman Cousins, Bill Fry, Art Buchwald, Alison Crane, Steve Allen, etc.) triggered the idea of this book in the first place.

I am conceptually indebted to Raymond Moody and Conrad Hyers. They are true pioneers in psychiatry and theology, and have confirmed my faith in the healing power of laughter.

I especially thank my typist/critic, Jeanne Wilkins, who has been patient, perceptive, and persistent. Her last directive in a list of "Dan's missions" to finish this book was, "Keep sense of humor intact!"

Dan Keller
January 1, 2000

PROLOGUE TO THE LAUGHTER FACTOR

by
Conrad Hyers

One may judge the importance of a book partly in terms of content and partly in terms of need. On both counts Dr. Keller's *The Laughter Factor* is important. There is a dearth of literature available to the psychotherapist that applies humor theory to humor therapy. Anyone who has done counseling surely senses that humor — on the part of both therapist and client — can be a significant ingredient in the healing process, yet few have given the matter systematic reflection and application. Freud made a preliminary effort in this direction in his *Wit and the Unconscious*, and Keller draws upon his study; but many aspects of the subject remained to be developed, especially the uses of humor by the counselor and client. *The Laughter Factor* amply rectifies this lacuna in our knowledge.

Before Freud, none other than the great American therapist Mark Twain credited healing powers to humor (and to his profession) when he wrote in *Tom Sawyer* of the old man who "laughed joyously and loud, shook up the details of his anatomy from head to foot, saying that such a laugh was money in a man's pocket because it cut down the doctor's bills like everything!" That, in essence, is what Keller's book is about, including a chapter on recent research indicating the various positive effects of shaking up the details of one's anatomy from head to foot in hearty laughter.

A book that might profitably be read in conjunction with

Keller's book is Ken Kesey's *One Flew Over the Cuckoo's Nest* which in its own way is also an exploration of the importance of humor — and of the lack thereof — in the context of psychotherapy. When the rabble-rousing, free-spirited Randall Patrick McMurphy is committed to the State Hospital for the Insane, his first impression is quite revealing of the disastrous effects of therapy without humor:

> That's the first thing that got me about this place, there wasn't anybody laughing. I haven't heard a real laugh since I came through that door . . . Man, when you lose your laugh you lose your footing.

There is an allegory here for the situation Keller's work aims to correct. Humor is an essential dimension of the whole and healthy personality. Without a well-developed sense of humor, something fundamental is missing; the corollary to that is illness. Humor involves the peculiarly human capacity to stand back and apart from one's situation, to see things more clearly and objectively — and also more honestly — and to take oneself and one's circumstances less seriously. There are many other positive functions of humor, but this one alone should have given humor greater attention than it has received.

The Laughter Factor provides a wealth of material that can be used in both ways: as part of the therapeutic process, but also as preventative exercise. One of the best features of the book is that it is not written in heavy jargonese, but is very readable and practical. The author does not fall into writing overly seriously about humor, and thus open himself to the charge that only those with little sense of humor are capable of writing books about it. Keller writes about humor with humor. And these are not theoretical proposals either; he has used humor and cultivated humor over years of counseling. And, judging from the many cases he cites, his various uses of humor in therapy have been very successful.

A helpful feature of the book is that so many examples and

suggestions are offered from the author's own experience in individual and group therapy. A sensitivity to the great variety of individual situations and needs is also much in evidence; a diversity of cases are cited, and in each case the technique is adapted to the individual. The frequent use of anecdotes from his own counseling gives not only concreteness to the text, but makes of it interesting reading. Most importantly, one can visualize many ways in which humor can be introduced and encouraged in one's own counseling.

In story after story, Keller proves his point. Humor really does make a difference. *The Laughter Factor* fills a void in the literature, and very readably so.

CONRAD HYERS

Conrad Hyers is the author of a number of books, including *Holy Laughter, The Meaning of Creation, Once Born, Twice Born Zen, Zen and the Comic Spirit, The Comic Vision,* and *The Laughing Buddha.* He chairs the Department of Religion at Gustavus Adolphus College and lectures on humor across the country.

CHAPTER I

GO AHEAD AND LAUGH

> "There are no things by which the troubles and difficulties of this life can be better resisted than with wit and humor."
>
> — H. K. Beecher

Humor's place in daily life has long been cherished. We humans like to laugh; the more heartily we laugh the better. Bill Cosby, Bette Midler, Gene Wilder, Carol Burnette, Sid Caesar, Bob Hope, Red Skelton, Groucho Marx, Will Rogers — Twain, Swift, Moliere, Plautus, Aristophanes — the clown, the mime, the court jester, the tribal trickster, etc., are but the hilarious tip of the iceberg. We know without thinking that "laughter is the best medicine." Our identity as a people would be bleakly bland without our humorists, comedians, and cartoonists. Why then, has humor's role in the world of therapy been so oddly neglected? Why is it that only of late has the paradox of taking humor seriously been taken seriously?

A reason may be that we have been so inundated with humor that we simply take humor for granted. That is, humor may be so innate a part of our "culture" that we don't give it a second thought. And there is no need to belabor the obvious in a psychiatric setting. But if humor *is* self-apparent, is it not an open window to the soul? Does it not provide us as immediate a view of the unconscious as the *body language* we are trained to see? Isn't the laughter that humor exhibits a language of the body itself? Can we not learn a lot from laughter's tone, context, frequency and intent? We as surely miss important insights when we take humor for granted.

Another reason humor is neglected is the nonsensical charm of its nature. That is, therapy is a kind of analysis; and humor displays a tongue-in-cheek resistance to being analyzed. Humor reads the blindness of reason to nonsense as a sickness. It evades being "pinned down" and explained like a specimen under a microscope. It knows that what makes life worth living is *felt* before it is thought. As studying too much theology can think God to death, too serious a scrutiny of humor can produce a corpse. We end up kicking the dead horse of "a concept" that bears little resemblance to what humor *is* when it's alive and well and kicking.

The same is true of therapists. We too often approach our work with the sobriety of a mortician. Intent on a "critical analysis" we dismiss humor as a diversion to be *seen through*. The message we thus convey is to *be serious and repress playful feelings*. Such a strategy amounts to treating a tapeworm by starving it to death. While destroying the disease, we rob its victim of his/her vital fluids. Humor, too, is a vital fluid. It does for the emotions what antibodies do for the body. It resists excessive sobriety and can be a patient's last defense against despair.

Therapy by the same token is serious business. The havoc that can be wrought by a frivolous approach to the likes of depression, anxiety, and suicide cannot be overstated. The therapist should *always* be sensitive to the depth of their seriousness. That the concerns of therapy are serious, however, does not exclude humor from the therapeutic process. It rather indicates humor's unquestioned importance. Because humor and seriousness are opposite sides of the same coin, they need each other to survive and go hand-in-hand. As Mark Twain puts it: "The secret source of humor is not joy but sorrow."[i] And where harmony is present the two are *intimately* connected. What follows is an exploration of that connection.

We will look first at clinical examples. These come from my own experience. They suggest humor's practical role in the process of healing. My choice of personal encounters as a starting point is on purpose. What, after all, keeps us honestly "in touch" but the incongruities of daily life? And few problems are as knotty or challenge us so directly as those that arise in therapy. They are the reason Freud reminds us that "pathography teaches the method."

Therapy, of course, is more immediate than any method. It requires a blood and guts response to stress in the spontaneity of the moment. Humor is similarly earthy. It tickles what hurts in a way that relieves the gravity of stress. Both humor and therapy intuit that to be wise is to be simple without being simplistic. So my examples are as concrete as I can make them. They depict reality in the raw, and are aimed as much at the layman as the clinician.

I then turn to ways to employ humor in a therapeutic setting. I explore attitude, style, and specific techniques that lend themselves to a humorous interaction. Each technique can be individually adapted. But they especially apply to groups because of humor's tendency to find a social outlet. There are, of course, countless ways to frame therapy in a humorous light. My suggestion to the reader is to follow your own instincts. I can't remember jokes, for example, and find them too "canned" to be helpful. So try methods that work for you and fit your own sense of humor.

My own list of humorous tactics includes: remembering to laugh, sharing embarrassing moments, role-playing, reading a chapter from a book, collecting cartoons, "fortune cookie" therapy, Norman Cousins tapes, movies, sitcoms, videos of comedians, etc. Comedians, by the way, should not be too shocking or hostile for the group to stand. They should be carefully chosen according to the needs and maturity of each patient. I've found Bill Cosby, Bob Newhart, Lilly Tomlin, and sometimes Father Sarducci, to be a great change of pace amidst the trauma of hospitalization. I've been surprised as well by the contagious effect on my part of a hearty laugh. Group members often mention that they enjoy hearing me laugh. A likely reason is that it gives them license to laugh in kind.

The methods I share are meant to support more orthodox approaches to psychological problems. They in no way replace the serious "reality-testing" that therapy requires. But I have no doubt that humor is every bit as important. My constant theme is how basic humor is to our human condition. I explore humor's relation to the likes of feeling, anxiety, tragedy, guilt, paradox, irony, laughter, wit, and the absurd.

The absurdity of life is not a joke to a patient in the grips of a suicidal depression. Yet the absurd can be "humored" and laughter is a needed tool for whittling absurdity's impact down to size. I think of Camus' reminder to imagine Sisyphus happy. "The absurd has reasons of its own," says Camus, but it has been demeaned to the level of "crippled reason."

Humor too is a kind of crippled reason with reasons of its own. And its role in daily life is too crucial to be dismissed as inappropriate, frivolous, or absurd. Freud makes the same point in his essay on humor as he faces Adolf Hitler and cancer of the jaw. I pray we're not as blind as the Nazis were to Freud — to the ethical corrective of healthy laughter. Yet our high-tech culture has literally pushed humor to the boundaries of *serious* consideration. If something is funny, it's "nonsense" and doesn't count. We thus deny ourselves the reverie of play that humor elicits.

I should quickly add that the strains of thought I pull together are *interdisciplinary*. I draw from psychiatry, philosophy, literature, theology, and my intent is holistic. Indeed, I believe that humor is a discipline in itself and should be studied at our universities — alongside Law, Medicine, Music, Art, etc. My sources include Freud, Nietzsche, Kierkegaard, Jung, Frankl, Suzuki, Beauvoir, Heidegger, Cosby, Hyers, Fanon, Becker, Laotse, Camus, May, Art Buchwald, Gilda Radner, Chris Rock, and others.

My last chapters are more personal. I explore the healing power of laughter in the loose ends of myself. Some of my disclosures were painful to state, yet they confirm my reasons for writing this book in the first place. Humor does buttress us amidst life's travails. And what is truly tragic can as surely be re-played at a later time as heartfelt laughter. Just as they once thought a return to balance of the four *humours* (blood, phlegm, cholor, and melancholy) was to be *in good humor*.

The secret to keeping bodily fluids in balance, naturally, was to laugh. Laughter (blood) in turn purged the body of apathy, anger, and melancholy. The only catch was that such laughter was dangerous if done in excess. That is, you could laugh too much, and then deplete yourself of cheerful confidence and turn good humor bad. This view held sway from the Middle Ages into the Renaissance. Because of the truth it contains, it's a shame that we left it behind. Whatever its anatomical flaws, the theory reflects the fluidity of humor in myself, and in many patients.

Laughter is also a unique feature of the human race. Its enjoyment separates *us* from the animals* and is as apparent as reason. The evolution of humor goes hand in hand with our ability to think. Not only are we the animal that thinks, we are the creature who laughs.

Oh my God! The therapy thinking requires may be as simple as *being funny*. Humor's role is to lighten the load that our grasp of complexity has heightened. It brings us down to earth and keeps us human. The bond in sound of humor, humus, and human speaks for itself here. Humor is a vital fluid in the soil of human survival. Or as Thurber puts it: "Humor is a serious thing. It is one of our greatest and earliest natural resources which must be preserved at all costs."[ii]

SANDY

I am often amazed, as a therapist, at humor's ability to resolve conflict when all else fails. I recall a couple who came to me at wit's end. Their adopted daughter was battling all attempts at commu-

---

* and might profoundly link us to them. Cf., Ashley Montagu's curious thesis (as developed in a lecture at the eighth annual conference of "The Power of Laughter and Play" in Dallas) that rediscovering such childhood traits as the need to laugh, love, and play may be intrinsic to "our evolution" of the human species.

nication. As professional educators, they were loaded with high-sounding reasons for Sandy's behavior. *In fact*, their intellectualizing was much of the problem. They could not relate to their daughter on an emotional level. They quickly refuted her logical contradictions without sensing the feelings behind them. Sandy, in turn, was frustrated to the point of rage at not being *heard*. She felt rejected and inferior for not being as adept with words as mom and dad. Being adopted compounded her inferior feelings and need to be "rescued." She was hell-bent on being whatever her parents were *not*.

Sandy was stubborn and blindly rebellious, and turned innocent remarks into the occasion of a power struggle. Having tried everything, I resorted to humor. I poked fun at her parents for being so rational and chuckled at Sandy when she took herself too seriously for her selfish britches. When defensive bickering struck me as ridiculous, I allowed myself the pleasure of a hearty laugh. The family responded with surprise, suspicion, and a curious glee. Why is this guy laughing? They began to enjoy my amusement. In a short time, tensions subsided and our communication got far more open. The breakthrough occurred when all three viewed their situation with humor.

Such encounters have convinced me of the need for the study that follows. I hope it's a catalyst for more books on how to use humor in therapy. To speak of "using" humor, of course, is heavy handed and crude. It is wrong to treat this special gift as a thing to be used as the means to any end. Like play, humor exists for no purpose beyond the free joy if its expression. It for sure surpasses any therapist's agenda. Yet therapy must carry this practical tension, and therapy can be kept honest by humor's presence.

Since therapy's aim is to heal pain, such pragmatism is justified. Therapy is an arena where one person helps another through a stressful situation. A good therapist has to be *practical* when the likes of suicide may weigh in the balance. He/she has no choice but to use humor, silence, kindness, or any tactic that intuitively works. To cling to a method that fails to respond flexibly to the crisis at hand is a serious mistake.

Humor curiously meets this standard. It is an energy, fluid enough in its relation to feeling, and practical in its laughter, to face and decipher our contradictions. Humor is smart and simple. It touches our common sense and our "courage to be." It helps us see the whole picture.

Merleau-Ponty, in contrast, sees therapy as an end game. If therapy is driven to its logical conclusion, he thinks, "a victor survives and a loser is driven to self-extinction." The number of suicides by psychiatrists and patients, supports this cynical view. Humor tempers the logic of such extremes. It disperses the intensity that a therapist, blind to humor, causes. As Jacob Riis notes: "The longer I live, the more I think of humor as in truth the saving sense."[iii] My words explore this sense in the light of healing. I hope your funny bone is tickled.

CHAPTER II

WELCOME TO THE FUNNY FARM

> "Humor is the shortest distance between two people."
> — Victor Borge

The following remark confirms my own sense of humor's role in the process of healing. It is made by the therapist of a withdrawn client who has been labeled a schizophrenic. She empathically writes:

> "The first ray of hope appeared when she began to use her own humor in response to mine. At first it was very sarcastic and self-depreciating, but gradually she developed a twinkle in her eyes, and as she regained her will to live, her use of humor became more positive; she began to laugh at herself, see humor in the worst situation, and tease me."[iv]

I am often amazed by the number of neuroses traceable to the family message that "nonsense will not be tolerated."

I'll bet this patient experienced such a death of humor and play in her formative years. The same was likely reinforced by a later crisis. It was then hidden and buried in layers of repression and busy-work. It now denounces the pleasure of play or uninhibited spontaneity as INAPPROPRIATE. At this level of awareness, the humorous interaction is just what the doctor ordered. When humor breaks through (= "breakthrough"), it is often dramatic. It can revive hope when sober styles of relating fail. There is a power in humor that can tip the delicate balance of our emotions from "Thanatos" toward "Eros."

MICHAEL

I remember a patient of whom this seemed especially true. Michael bore a physical resemblance to Groucho Marx. But the similarity stopped there. He was barely able to say hello. His frozen position was sitting in a corner looking dejected for hours on end. As I got to know Michael better, I discovered a dry wit that his "flat affect" tended to complement. Both his wit and visual appearance were a natural part of his personality. Because of his depression, however, he was blind to how witty he truly was.

During a clumsy attempt at communication on my part, Michael mumbled something I couldn't understand. "Come again," I said. He replied flatly, "I'd like to, but I don't think I can." Surprised by his witty remark, I spontaneously laughed. Michael enjoyed my response. And noting *his* pleasure at my pleasure, I said, "That's cute, Michael, real cute." He replied, "Thank you, I always try to please." In accepting Michael's wit, I was accepting him.

From this exchange of slapstick evolved a mutual trust. It was my first inkling of enough strength on Michael's part to cope with his depression. As his mood brightened, his ability both to laugh, and offer humor to others, remarkably increased. To the delight of staff and patients alike, he felt free enough eventually to give his imitation of Groucho Marx. "Close, but no cigar," he would say while flicking his cigar in the ashtray. I clearly saw that expressing humor was essential to Michael's well being. It was at the heart of Michael's considerable intelligence. Humor was a forgotten part of his personality, of which he needed to be reminded.

MILDRED

Another use of laughter is in freeing the taboos and repressed content of sexual guilt. I recall a discussion in one of my groups of Woody Allen's "Everything You Wanted to Know About Sex But Were Afraid To Ask." Mildred was a pious prude whose self-righteous air was driving her peers batty. She naturally "saw nothing of value in the film." Even so, she opened up a lot after its viewing. In the group discussion that followed, she spoke with animation of her parents' attitude toward sex. She linked a childhood lecture from her mother on having "dirty thoughts" to the failure of her marriage. She even joined in the group's laughter at a patient's description of the sheep scene.

The movie was a clear catalyst of Mildred's growth. Less self-righteous, she grew open to sincere attempts at understanding her situation. She dropped the pretentions that so infuriated her peers. She was more honest with her feelings, and her anger in particular. She connected how she was raised with her present depression.

Laughter and the film's discussion triggered self-reflection. It enabled Mildred to view her sexual past with humor and in a balanced perspective. She talked freely of felt inadequacies, imagined and real. Laughter sparked her courage to vent a truckload of neurotic guilt. In place of rejection, her peers responded with empathy and acceptance. This opened the possibility in Mildred of self-acceptance. The group was as pleased as Mildred with the breakthrough that occurred.

MARTIN

A like insight came to me from a patient after shock treatment. He calmly remarked: "That was a truly electrifying experience." I do not mean to minimize the seriousness of being depressed enough to receive ECT or its effect on the brain. But note the role of humor here: first, as a way the patient can claim his humanity and say to the world, "I am still alive"; and second, as an emotional outlet for an intolerable double bind.

Martin was in a Catch-22 position. He did not want shock treatment, but saw no other solution to his depression. Even so, he could make light of his situation and his crazy options. Martin proved that through humor the absurdity of the human condition can be *communicated*. When we are trapped by conditions beyond our control, humor can be a source of comfort. In Martin's case, humor was an escape valve for feelings in need of expression.

WALTER

Humor can also be a first step in broaching uncomfortable and painful memories. I remember a patient from a small Georgia town. Walter had been hospitalized for an annoying habit to wide-eyed spinsters across the street. He retrieved his newspaper every morning in the buff.

I tried a low-keyed approach to the matter. This included my affirmation of Walter's unique, albeit bizarre and hostile, sense of humor. Walter was able to say with a straight face: "I always forget to put my pants on." In a literal sense, Walter was right. Just as important, his comment was funny. I was tickled and responded with incredulous laughter.

As I noted without judgment, the actual humor of his problem, I saw Walter improve. In time, he spoke of motives of rage at his aunt and stepmother. Walter had not previously admitted his rage even to himself. The use of humor made an exploration of repressed memories possible. It relieved vulnerabilities that a more "objective" approach to his behavior would have crushed. Instead of saying in the "Dragnet mentality" of Joe Friday, "Give me the facts, ma'am, nothing but the facts," the therapist, via an openness to humor, can say, "I'm ready and willing to hear your story."

JASON

I think of a stuttering and nearly catatonic client in his early twenties. Jason stubbornly resisted all attempts at communication. His silence and penetrating gaze cast an inhibiting shadow on the group. He clearly intimidated more reticent peers. During a very humorous exchange, however, Jason opened up dramatically.

He blurted without solicitation, "Have any of you ever seen things that aren't real?" What followed was a remarkable admission of hallucinations that up to this point he had carefully hidden. Jason reported, among other things, receiving verbal directives from a spider outside his window. He further claimed to have seen a giant Visine bottle on his front lawn. The image was funny, and some laughed. Humor catalyzed Jason's decision to trust the group with his fantastic apparitions. It helped him conquer his fears and even find humor in the group's response to a giant Visine bottle.

I approached Jason's bizarre descriptions with a grain of salt. This proved helpful. He stopped dwelling on the abnormalities of his imagination so intensely. By casting his hallucinations in the light of humor, they were disarmed of their scary fascination. They could then be manageably traced to an emotional source.

Group members responded in kind. They shared less dramatic breaks with reality — a common experience — and linked them to stress, culture shock, fear, and isolation. "I needed a friend, so I invented one in my head to keep me company," said Helen, in a supportive way. Humor's proximity to repressed feeling is what prompted this encounter.

Another basic role of humor in therapy is the rejuvenation of the therapist. Humor is welcome relief from the transference and hostility to which the therapist is often exposed. Rejuvenation is especially possible in settings with a caring and mutually supportive staff. The private sharing of a good laugh at the behavior of an obstreperous patient is essential. It helps the professional keep his equilibrium. He/she can thus respond more humanely to a volatile situation.

TURNER

I recall a patient who was abusive, hostile, and physically aggressive. Turner also had the peculiar habit of hiding large supplies of prune juice under his bed. Identifying feces with the devil, Turner felt the need to purify his bowels with obsessive regularity. So prune juice, pilfered in bulk from the kitchen, became a life-and-death commodity. Being able to laugh with fellow staff at Turner's ridiculous obsession was an important outlet for coping with his tantrums. It fostered a patient and more flexible response to hostile behavior that couldn't otherwise have been tolerated. By keeping a humorous perspective, I affirmed Turner as a person and avoided having to place him in isolation. Humor tempered an over-reaction to his psychotic delusions.

The sharing of humor with staff, in other words, encouraged an empathic penetration of paranoid defenses. These defenses were present in Turner for good reason — a mean, violent father who time and again betrayed Turner's trust. Even so, there is something funny about construing prune juice as contraband. As Turner began to see the humor of his behavior, moreover, his fixation subsided. Also, he was more able to trust others.

I don't mean to imply that Turner was cured overnight or that his symptoms of paranoia weren't taken seriously. Coaxing Turner out of his isolation was a long and tedious process. His treatment required patience, empathy, and turning the other cheek. As crucial to his recovery was an undaunted sense of humor.

HERNANDEZ

Humor is also helpful in taming violence. I think of a fourteen-year-old sociopath with homicidal leanings. Hernandez was seething with rage and aggressively narcissistic. Saying hello could provoke overturned tables, flying chairs, broken vases, etc. Such outbursts wreaked havoc on the unit and buoyed his belief in his own omnipotence. His tactics of intimidation included scorn, sarcasm, pouting, verbal threats, and loud temper tantrums. He enjoyed scaring his peers. He was also fiercely gay. Hernandez loudly bragged of his escapades as a "disco queen" in a male nightclub and of "whoring for scratch."

I had no illusions at this point of "curing" Hernandez. He was possessed of a rage that was too deeply rooted, and my only goal was to temper his explosive behavior. I responded to insults with concern and as much patience as I could muster. And I refused to let Hernandez put me on the defensive. That would only fuel the power struggle he hoped to incite. I deflected insults by being indirect. If he lambasted me in group for asking a simple question, I replied, "Excuse me for asking," and then calmly persisted. When he called me a "money-sucking, honky head-shrinker," I said "Thank you" and wondered aloud why he was so angry.

Hernandez slowly came around. He realized I was not the enemy and was as hard a nut to crack as he. He talked bitterly of his father who had physically abused and abandoned him at an early age. He described a symbiotic bond to his mother that bordered on incest (e.g., sleeping in her bed until the age of 12). His mother in turn called Hernandez her "little man" and had spoiled him rotten. Hernandez readily admitted this fact. The Oedipal mix of mom's overindulgence and a hatred of his father had created a selfish monster. Hernandez believed he had enough power to drive his father from home and keep his mother for himself.

What enabled me to soften Hernandez' wrath was a kind answer firmly grounded in humor. Although nearly illiterate, Hernandez was verbal, slick, and street-wise smart. He thought life was absurd and had a grasp of the humorous essentials. As I pondered the absurdity of the life that Hernandez was forced to live, I found the empathy and humor that his treatment required.

The sharing of my own sense of the absurdity of life was a breakthrough. It helped Hernandez see that he wasn't unique in his knowledge of the absurd. And it instilled in Hernandez the self-acceptance that humor inspires. More to the point, if Hernandez could not in an absurd sense reconcile his rage, his future was doomed. If he couldn't learn to control his temper, he'd become a ward of the state in a prison. Developing an absurd sense of humor was a matter of personal survival. Hernandez couldn't change the formative years of his life; but he could laugh at their absurd meaning.

The more I worked with Hernandez, the more humor entered our conversations. Clearly, as Hernandez experienced the vulnerability that humor's enjoyment allows, he got more *reflective*. His positive effect on his peers was surprising, and he explored their problems in group in a sensitive way. I hope Hernandez is doing well and that he remembers the necessity of a sense of humor.

BUFORD

Buford was a burly "mountain boy" from north Georgia who carved skin from his arm to express his feelings. His use of words was literal and bluntly concrete. Because of a low I.Q., Buford had a limited capacity for humor. But he could be reached via direct questions and overt concern.

Assured of not being *laughed at*, Buford allowed me entrance to his paranoid world. I noticed he liked cartoons and that he laughed aloud at Mr. Magoo and the Flintstones. So I laughed too. Seeing I could laugh at things that struck him as funny, was to Buford a source of glee. An amazing increase in trust resulted.

Withholding inappropriate laughter was similarly instructive. When Buford laughed at a nurse sitting on spilled orange juice, I coughed gruffly and sternly stared. *Not laughing* sensitized Buford to what hurt people and what did not. "That's not funny, Buford," I said. "How would you like it if someone did that to you?" He slowly grasped that the difference between humor and cruelty was how he would like to be treated himself. If Buford's humor was as dumb as The Three Stooges, it was better than no humor at all. It brought comic relief and moments of play that assured Buford he could trust me. And humor helped me to like Buford, despite his crude demeanor.

KARL

I think of a professor who requested counseling "for no particular reason." When Karl mentioned in a session that "I enjoy being austere with my students," I probed further. He soon stated, "I can scare people with my mind. It makes me feel superior." I explored the word "feel" because feeling was clearly what Karl lacked. Our discussion turned to childhood and Karl admitted "never fitting in" and being a "loner." He related telling scenes of rejection by his peers with a tone of disdain and intellectual indifference.

Karl's parents had punished him in humiliating ways. If these memories were painful, he didn't show it. Yet Karl's fierce denial of "any pain at all," proved his pain's existence. Every sentence Karl spoke was crisp, erudite and smugly detached. He had found solace as a child by always acting like an adult. Karl was "the brain of the family" and avoided emotional attachment by hiding in a book. He learned to get his way with his classmates with sarcastic intimidation. I once asked him if he remembered laughing as a child. Karl answered as if smelling a rotten egg. He said, "No, I don't ever recall really laughing." Karl was a control freak, ill at ease with humor. Humor was a sharp reminder of his childhood and being laughed at.

I took Karl seriously without treating him with kid gloves. That is, I took him seriously enough not to take his seriousness seriously. My approach was also the safest for me, because Karl could be vicious with his tongue. He was a bit like a vulture eating Prometheus' liver "for no particular reason." Humor was a needed elixir for him and for me.

HILDA, MIKE, DAVE, MARY, ETC.

Other examples of humor in therapy are too numerous to mention. A widowed oldster is trying to make a new life for herself. Humor gives Hilda the courage to survive the loss of her husband and spurs a sense of independence. A suicidal man of thirty still lives with his mother (and in her shadow). My use of humor, and Mike's humorous response, lays the groundwork for a trusting encounter. A deeper penetration of his problems then evolves. An adolescent sees his mother kill his father in self-defense. Humor eases Dave's rage and pain. A woman carries the guilt of incest with her father. A humorous exchange leads Mary to the insight that as tragic as incest is, it is not the end of the world. She becomes more playful and sees that fun does not ordain seduction. Etc., etc., etc.

The best candidates for humor are people who are funny by nature. But amidst a crisis, tragedy, or stress, they have lost touch with their sense of humor. Often paralyzed by fear in the shadow of a depression, they won't let humor surface. Yet such people are also lucky. Because in rediscovering their sense of humor, they find an inner strength that leads to healing. They may also feel the liberation of finding what they thought was lost. They experience a new appreciation of their sense of humor.

CAROL AND JOAN

Gerald Piaget has written me of a similar example. It is striking because unexpected anger triggers a breakthrough that coincides with laughter. He writes:

> Two or three years ago I had occasion to treat a young woman suffering from a rather advanced case of metastatic melanoma. This 38-year-old wife and mother of two had entered therapy for other reasons; however, with the recurrence of her cancer, her fear and depression became severe. To further complicate matters, my wife and Carol were best of friends. During the following months, humor played an important role in the work Carol and I did together. Carol had a rich, well-developed sense of humor, which she put to good use in the course of her therapy. It was natural to ask

Carol if any of my humor tactics had been particularly helpful. Carol looked at me for a minute, and then grinned. "No offense, Gerry," she said, "but nothing we've done in therapy holds a candle to what Joan (my wife) said to me on the phone last week while you were out of town." "Oh," I said, barely able to contain my excitement. "Tell me about it." "Well, I was feeling horrible. You were gone, my husband was in no mood to hear more bitching, and I was really depressed. So I called Joan to talk. During our conversation, I mentioned that with the cancer, and the depression, and the uncertainty and all, maybe there was no use in going on. I said it sort of casually, but in truth thoughts of suicide had been coming up for a couple of days. Now, Joan knows I'm not the suicidal type, but she got *really* angry at me." "Damn it, Carol," she yelled. "If you *dare* kill yourself I swear I'll go to that cemetery and piss all over your grave!" Carol chuckled, remembering. "I was so surprised I didn't know what to say. Then I just started laughing and couldn't stop." "Another thing," she went on, "That image hasn't worn off, at least not yet. You know this hasn't been a very good week for me. But whenever I think of killing myself, I get this ridiculous image of Joan out there in the graveyard, with her eyes angry and her lower lip stuck out and her skirt hiked up around her waist, just squatting there on my grave . . . It lightens me up. I just don't feel like dying anymore. I sure hope it lasts." Carol and I discussed this experience in detail and were able to use variations on the graveyard image productively during therapy. Unquestionably, the experience was of value to Carol in a variety of ways. She got immediate relief from her depressive feelings and suicidal thoughts. She got a powerful associated image that helped her avoid suicidal ideation and maintain a positive perspective. And she got a boost regarding some power/dependency issues that centered around her relationship with her therapist.

Gerry's wit and analysis appreciated, there is another telling theme in his example. Namely, the acceptance of death in the context of affirming life. Humor, if it is genuine, is entirely compatible with such affirmation. It says "yes" to life despite tragedy and despite the fact that each one of us dies. It hopes beyond the grave and transcends despair. It celebrates life in the face of death by claiming the courage to laugh. On the lighter side, humor is a lot more fun and honest than giving up.

CHAPTER III

THE ANATOMY OF A CHORTLE

> "The art of medicine lies in amusing the patient while nature cures the disease."
> — Voltaire

If there's a funny bone or not, I don't know. But a serious question is laughter's effect on the body. What happens, when our cheeks blush and our belly shakes the spasm of a guffaw, is more than a good feeling. Our vocal cords are sounding an elixir as old as Solomon's praise of "a merry heart." And modern medicine tells us that we are measurably cleansing our somatic pores.

We now know that laughter catalyzes the endocrine system. Our pituitary gland releases pain-reducing chemicals. Endorphins and enkephalins trigger the sensation of pleasure. Hormones called catecholamines heighten our alertness. Our heart rate increases. Our pulse leaps from 60 to 120 beats per minute. Our bodily organs are being exercised. Oxygen is being rushed to our toes and fingers. Our diaphragm and muscles are being contracted and toned. Our lungs thrust air from the mouth as fast as 60 miles per hour. The region of our brain that "creates" turns electrically active. Our right brain and source of emotion is working (playing?) in harmonious tandem with its cognitive opposite. All of the above "happens" as tears of joy water our eyes. We are just scratching the surface of the boon to the body of a hearty laugh.

Consider the aforementioned tears of joy. We sense instinctively that it's healthy to shed tears. Crying is a needed emotional release. It's curious that pain, pleasure, and sometimes rage, can trigger a tear. Tears and emotion are closely linked, and medicine has begun to prove it. Tears caused by *emotion*, and oddly *not* those caused by an onion, contain two chemicals with specific functions. These chemicals are leucine-enkephalin and prolactin. Leucine-enkephalin is an endorphin that numbs pain with pleasure.

Tears also contain toxins and clean the body. A symptom of stress is the accumulation of toxins in the body. A reason men have more stress-related diseases than women may be that men cry less. It follows that there is a physical link between reducing stress and shedding tears when we laugh.

A subject I think medicine should study is the relationship of laughter and life span.* I wonder if it can be shown that people who laugh more tend to live longer. My hunch is that this is the case. Laughter is an immediate outlet of tension, and seems to resist disease (dis-ease) with positive emotions. Laughter also conquers timidity by taking a risk, and studies have shown that "risk takers" do live longer. Who knows? Perhaps laughter has a similar effect. I offer "Bunny" as an example.

BUNNY

While completing this book, I was subjected to a three-week houseguest, a Mrs. Bunny Klopper from Iowa. Bunny was the 82-year-old mother of a former colleague. I felt put upon, and was grumpy in our first encounters, because my wife was on vacation with her sister in Greece, the air conditioner was broken, and I had a deadline to finish the book. I was not a happy camper. But what I feared would be a chore turned out to be a blessing in disguise.

At the prompting of her daughter, Bunny had decided "to fly

---

* Cf., A humor-inducing handbook by the Ethel Percy Andrus Gerontology Center in Los Angeles that includes cartoons, limericks, books, records, and movies as a medicant for the elderly.

to Atlanta for a change of pace." She was adjusting to the death of her husband and a brother, and respected my space. Between brief encounters in the kitchen or on the porch, I discovered Bunny to be the spunkiest octogenarian I've ever met. She walked a mile every morning despite the heat. She was more good-natured than me about enjoying each day of life; she possessed a delightful sense of humor.

Bunny called laughter "the only way to go" and pitied elderly friends "who think they're over the hill and shrivel up like they're already dead." Bunny was an avid reader. She spent her 80th birthday in Morocco visiting a school for the deaf and dumb for which she was raising money. She liked Mozart, jazz, and modern music. I was amazed when she survived ten hours of sightseeing, from which I was exhausted, with the *esprit de corps* of a trooper.

That hot Atlanta day included four flights of stairs at the High Museum of Art, a standing room only view of a children's dance group, a half-mile trek to a concert in Piedmont Park (at which we sat on the ground), a tour of Emory University, and an Ethiopian dinner filled with lively conversation. We talked about everything under the sun, from how times had changed, to Bunny's appearance on "The Today Show" for being the oldest person in a walkathon. "I'm proud of my age," she said, "and I think it's funny that people are shy about asking me how old I am." We laughed loudly and often throughout the day.

No, I haven't asked for Bunny's hand in marriage. But it's not out of the question. I mention Bunny because she confirms my hunch that longevity is a bodily function of a merry heart. *The Anatomy of an Illness* by Norman Cousins is similarly convincing.

NORMAN COUSINS

Cousins attributes his victory over a crippling collagen disease (ankylosing spondylitis) to faith, hope, confidence, vitamin C and "the joyous discovery that ten minutes of genuine belly laughter would give me at least two hours of pain-free sleep." Cousins credits his cure to the Marx Brothers, Candid Camera, and a physician with a sense of humor.

Cousins' illness was very serious. He was given "a chance in 500" of recovery. His symptoms included arthritic pain, nodules, "gravel-like" substances under the skin, difficulty turning in bed, a red cell sedimentation count of 115, periodic paralysis of the jaw, and a pain in the lower spine in the first stages of disintegration. As Cousins puts it: "The bones in my spine and practically every joint in my body felt as though I had been run over by a truck."

Yet Cousins conquers his disease amidst his discovery of *the will to live*. He reasons that as negative emotions — stress, rage, depression, fear — have a negative effect on the body, so positive emotions — courage, love, hope, joy — must have a positive effect. At the top of his list is the felt relief of heartfelt laughter. Cousins echoes Kant's view of laughter as a "feeling of health" that can "reach the body through the soul and use the latter as the physician of the former."*

The task of the physician called a psychiatrist, of course, is soul (*Psyche*) healing (*Iatreia*). He/she attempts this task in the context of the body; and if Cousins is right, any psychiatrist worth his/her salt should have a grasp of the healing power of the positive emotions. In what similar sense does laughter mediate between *soma* and *psyche*? Is it more than coincidence that the diaphragm both differentiates *the heart* from the lower functions of the abdomen and is the muscle of inspiration (breath = spirit or *pneuma* in Greek) that gives rise to laughter?

Does psychiatry need to evolve a corresponding model of laughter? Are there ways to distinguish laughter that comes from the heart (hearty laughter), laughter that vents the spleen (or slings mud), and ironical laughter that smugly echoes the "height" of condescension? And should therapy shape a less mechanical view of laughter that reflects humor's role in the play of the unconscious?

---

* Cf., the addition of "The Lively Room" at De Kalb General Hospital in Atlanta whose sole purpose is to induce laughter.

Another medical discovery is laughter's release of muscular tension. When we laugh, our muscles (and especially the diaphragm) tensely contract and cathartically relax. Thus laughter is a kind of exercise — or "inner jogging" — that tones and strengthens our bodies. The more robustly we laugh, the more dramatic the effect. Hearty laughter includes an electrical stimulation of the skin akin to sexual excitement.

Many studies show that humor and play are closely linked to sexual pleasure. There is, after all, an orgasmic side to laughter. What laughter and sex have in common is: uninhibited spontaneity, letting go of control, repetitive spasms of pleasure, a felt release of tension, a flagellation of tangible gasps, a liberation of pain that happiness conquers, a ritual of foreplay that is vulnerably felt, the individuation of a basic need, a shared celebration of self-acceptance, a bond with "the other," a freed moment of trust, a brief transcendence of death, a repressed wish expressed, the communication of care, a flushing of the face, tears of joy, etc.

Clearly, couples who can laugh together are more sexually fulfilled. The proximity of cells in the neo-cortex of pleasure and pain is similarly curious. Also, anger disrupts the mutuality of erotic pleasure that humor enhances. Laughter's emotional link to physiology again arises.*

Jane and Robert Brody have written delightful articles on the connection of body and emotion. Robert speaks convincingly of gelotology (the study of laughter, or *gelos,* in Greek) as if it were a discipline — on the order of ontology, seismology, or archeology. Jane has written on the curious chemistry of the likes of hiccups and yawning. There is something laughable in the choice of such topics.

Ms. Brody notes that "yawning is induced by observing someone else's yawn." She adds the amazing insight that "people who are acutely ill yawn less while their condition remains serious, and psychotic individuals hardly ever yawn." Yawning, in short, is healthy and contagious. It is freely enjoyed. What is true of yawn-

---

* See W. F. Fry's "Psychodynamics of Sexual Humor" in Medical Aspects of Human Sexuality (Sept., 1974).

ing — including "an exaggerated intake of oxygen-rich air" — is also true of laughing.

Medicine links laughter to an increased capacity of the lungs to oxygenate blood. Laughter triggers a cleansing of the circulatory system from the lobes of our ears to the tips of our toes. Laughter also speeds the process of digestion; there is some evidence that laughter is a laxative. Thus the phrase "farting around" may have a biological basis.

James Wandersee defines laughter biologically as:

> ... a spontaneous motor reflex of 15 facial muscles in a coordinated, stereotyped contraction pattern accompanied by altered breathing. If the lifting muscle of the upper lip (zygomatic major) is stimulated by electrical currents of increasing strength, facial expressions from smile to grin to convulsive laughter are produced. Although it starts as a motor reflex in infants, as socialization occurs voluntary control of laughter is gradually substituted for spontaneous reflex activity.[v]

Wandersee adds that humor helps students learn because: 1) it eases the tension between student and teacher and helps to establish rapport; 2) it maximizes the level of attention; and 3) it fosters a classroom climate "conducive to creative assimilation." His most telling point is that when humor is present in learning, we remember what we've learned both better and longer. He thinks the synapses of the brain that link pleasure and memory are triggered when we laugh.

We can now map the bicameral fluctuations of laughter in the brain. Both the right and left brain turn electrically active (Svebak) and work in tandem. The flow of EEG alpha waves is concurrently balanced between the lobes. It's as if the right and left brain "get the joke" together. Laughter circuits "a brief fusion" of the opposite sides of the brain. The synapses of the brain experience an equilibrium of electrical associations. We are actually speaking with medical precision when we say, "I got a charge out of that."

I haven't mentioned the adrenaline laughter spreads through the nervous system or the exercise it gives the mouth, jaws, vocal cords, abdomen, and facial muscles. Our face contracts like a pretzel as if venting pain. Alison Crane notes that laughter, depending on how hard, how long, and how often we laugh, discernibly lowers blood pressure. It strengthens the heart, and improves circulation and respiration. Also, there is a biochemical component to laughter that fights depression and perhaps cancer.

I am not pushing laughter as a cure for cancer, although many studies show an emotional factor in the body's resistance to cancer and other diseases. My milder claim is that honing a sense of humor is a kind of preventive medicine. It buoys our resistance. Just as physical exercise makes us more robust, heartfelt joy is a needed antidote for what makes us feel ill.

Exuberant laughter *does* trigger the brain's release of a hefty charge of endorphins whose molecular structure resembles morphine. Endorphins are linked to pleasure centers in the brain that free us of stress. We know that stress causes muscle tension, chronic fatigue, hypertension, migraine headaches, and a host of physical problems. Stress also harms the immune system by flooding our blood with corticosteroids from the adrenal gland. Corticosteroids become "cortisol" and decrease our resistance to colds, heart attacks, and carcinogenic cells. Laughter remarkably lowers the level of cortisol in our blood. It follows that laughter is a remedy for stress.[vi]

Laughter's stimulation of the immune system is more striking still. Laughter increases and activates T lymphocytes and T cells with helper/suppresser receptors. T cells work in tandem with neurotransmitters sent from the brain that "tell" mobilized immune cells what infection to attack. At the same time, laughter prompts an increased number of "natural killer cells" into action. More independent than T cells, natural killer cells (NK) are a bit like the body's Green Berets. NK cells attack lethal cells on their own and are directly fatal to pernicious intruders. They enable a healthy immune system, with the help of laughter and similar emotions, to do its job.[vii]

Laughter's activation of saliva is even touted as a healing agent, because laughter and joy stimulate salivary immunoglobulin A. And IgA is the throat's first line of defense against contagious invaders.[viii] More impressive is our discovery that the brain is the most prolific gland in the body. We once thought the brain secreted a few hormones. We now know that the brain produces over 2,000 biochemical secretions — and probably many more. These occur in direct response to emotion and what we think, imagine, and feel. They should at least remind us: "A merry heart doeth good like medicine." (Proverbs 17:22)

CHAPTER IV

TRICKS OF THE TRADE

"Cured yesterday of my disease,
I died last night of my physician."
— Matthew Prior

There are tricks of the trade in therapy that encourage humor's occurrence. To employ such tricks opens the therapist to a dynamic he/she doesn't fully control or understand. If controlling the client is his/her only goal, he'd best avoid humor altogether, because humor is unpredictably honest, and it resists rigid manipulation in a healthy way. I've found being open to humor, almost without exception, to have been worth the risk. I'll cite some examples and methods that have worked for me.

A good friend sometimes draws cartoons of his patients during their sessions. Jay is an excellent psychiatrist and very conscientious. His clinical aim is to portray the patient's predicament in a non-threatening way. Jay can't tell me why his cartoons work but is sure that they do. He reports the discovery by his patients of "aha" insights that his cartoons trigger. A picture really is worth a thousand words, and we remember what we SEE. Jay's creative empathy via a cartoon is a personal "snapshot" of a patient's situation. He thinks his cartoons spur imaginative access to obvious problems that are often denied.

Jay's skills as a clinician go far beyond drawing cartoons, although he may be a frustrated cartoonist. Jay is shrewd, patient, empathic, moral, and didactic. He is also funny and witty and freely laughs. He is kind and listens and knows the role humor plays in the process of healing. In group therapy Jay combines humor with insight in ingenious ways. His use of humor prompts his patients to get actively involved in their own solutions. Jay's refreshing approach includes cartoons.

DENNIS

A patient named Dennis let me see the cartoons that Jay had sketched. Dennis valued the cartoons as maps of growth and self-awareness. Each cartoon is dated and reflects current issues in the course of his treatment. Several cartoons reveal introverted repression. Their theme is a need to express gut-level feelings. One shows a rabbit tiptoeing through the underbrush. A bright sun is surveying the scene. The sun is winking and has a smile on its face. Oblivious to the merry sun, the shy rabbit mumbles, "There must be a better way to get what I want." Another shows the arms of a person, hidden behind a door, throwing a briefcase full of papers across the room. He's shouting: "Screw it." The caption below reads: "HOW NOT TO HAVE A HARD TIME DROPPING IT." Jay's cartoons depict a workaholic with trouble showing any anger.

A man with glasses is wrapped in a ream of papers that even cover his mouth. They form an endless list of things to do. "Salt, gas, shave, file, dictate, laundry, closet, vacuum, study, ad lib, etc." The headline above reads: "SOMEWHERE I MISSED THE NINETIES." Another cartoon shows a squashed executive in a suit and tie, trying to crawl forward with a desk on his back. The caption below reads: "THERE MUST BE A BETTER WAY TO MOVE ALL THAT PAPERWORK."

Recurring themes are isolation and a self-imposed burden of time. A crowned king is sitting on a throne and has a large clock for a face. A drop of perspiration creases his brow. Jay resists being funny, and lists the basic human needs of "NURTURE, ACCEPTANCE, REASSURANCE, AND VALIDATION." The next cartoon is of a shipwrecked survivor on a deserted island. The survivor has a pencil in his hand and is making another list. His only companion is a tree with a single coconut about to fall. Jay's quote captures his client's obsessive-compulsive traits. It reads, "Gawd, how will I ever find time to get this coconut ready for Thanksgiving?" The same theme is captured via the epitaph on Dennis' tombstone. His epitaph is a list of "things to do." A witness admiringly remarks: "Still . . . there's something impressive in all that work."

Another cartoon portrays problems in Dennis' social life. Or rather, it shows that Dennis has no social life at all. Father Time is dressed as a hippie and carrying a placard of protest. The placard reads: "MAKE LOVE NOW BEFORE IT'S TOO LATE." Although very successful, Dennis had no girlfriend and no close friends. He was a meticulous lawyer who had structured his life around nothing but work. Dennis was obsessed with avoiding the vulnerability that intimacy requires. Jay's last cartoon very clearly makes this point.

Two mountain climbers are scaling the granite face of a Buddha. Hidden within the mountain is an "Attorney-At-Law" scribbling words on a piece of paper. A carrier pigeon, with a question mark above its head, has a letter in its beak. The pigeon is confused by who should receive the letter. A straining climber shouts: "They assure me he runs *the* efficient office."

Jay insists that Dennis has made progress and that his cartoons have been a helpful tool. Jay's cartoons convey in a visual way what "cheap talk" does not. Their use of humor is non-threatening, laughable, and directly honest. They are also a tangible gift that conveys Jay's identification with his client's condition.

Another method is simply sharing embarrassing moments. This is especially helpful in groups and encourages reticent members to "let their hair down." The usual outcome is spontaneous laughter over what was once a painful situation. If sharing embarrassing moments yields nothing but comic relief, it is worthwhile, because comic relief is no small feat when feeling overwhelmed. It importantly includes "letting go" of burdensome defenses. There is the discovery that what was once a mortifying moment can be collectively enjoyed. Also present is the frank admission that we are all human.

Merely mentioning humor can be a medicant. When making a presentation on the subject to patients or staff, I am often amazed at the flood of personal examples it elicits. Giving credence to humor in therapy clearly frees the patient of awkward inhibitions. It gives him/her license to enjoy those impulses that too much sobriety censors. Paradoxically, humor often complements the exploration of more serious themes.

When humor occurs, the therapist should acknowledge and affirm it. The next step is to gently explore the insights that humor evolves. I say gently because too heavy-handed a response will inhibit the progress made and can be internalized as a betrayal of trust.

KIM

I think of a client who was fragile and very bright. Extremely anxious, Kim had experienced the trauma of being raped at gunpoint. In the course of treatment I asked her to evaluate certain sections of this book. She mentioned later that some of its content was helpful to her recovery. She also shared examples of humor in her own therapy. I felt humbled and affirmed by Kim's openness. For she knew the subject from the inside out and in the light of suffering I would never know. Kim's insights would have remained stillborn if I hadn't shared my fondness of humor.

Another approach is to remind the patient of childhood moments of heartfelt laughter. I have been surprised by the universality of such moments *regardless of personal history*. I remember laughing myself at the age of eight with a childhood friend — to the point of tears while falling to the floor. This happened in front of a curious adult who had no idea what it was we were laughing at. I don't remember myself. But the event was an undeniable source of pleasure. The therapist can help the patient reconstruct the felt impact of such pleasure. As the seeds of depression and guilt reside in early trauma, so the potential for enjoying life lies in the self's earliest actualization of joy. The simple recollection of pleasurable memories can trigger associations that clarify the present as a source of strength.

Such memories ground the patient in playful impulses whose origin lies in childhood. These impulses stand in opposition to the reality principle and amount to a nonsensical submersion in the original humours of joy. They occasionally surface, umbilical cord and all, and trigger an instinctive return to humorous themes. They can be instrumental in overcoming deep-rooted fears. Because humor is closely linked to the movement toward affirmation that painful memories tend to repress. Too rigid an attempt to explore pain may lead to hopeless resignation. It can open a Pandora's box of humiliation, rage, and blame that seems impossible to overcome.

Humor, in contrast, neutralizes the pull of Thanatos. It reminds the patient of a personal past that can as clearly be replayed in the key of pleasure. Humor's deeper origin lies in the innocence of childhood that it freely enjoys. No matter how much pain a child absorbs, he/she carries self-contained pockets of contentment that are life affirming. The energy these reserves tap is that of Eros. And they can be drawn on as a strength in the light of humor. Real excitement occurs when patient and therapist walk the path of humor's inspiration.

The therapist's willingness to be fallible, and even make a fool of himself, is at this point crucial. A spontaneous exchange of humor requires a high level of trust without the fear of being judged. When I am too afraid of making a mistake, I implant a like fear in the patient that inhibits communication. Socrates was right in this regard. Self-knowledge, no matter how perceptive, means being open to one's own ignorance. I have thus found stumbling through a session without pretension to be an effective method of treatment. What does it matter if my patients discover that I am a less than perfect human being? Such a discovery may even be central to their own self acceptance. It certainly relieves *in me* a self-imposed burden of infallibility, which in any final analysis is ridiculous.

I am not afraid to share my eccentricities with my patients, especially when it thwarts a patient's wish to perceive me as a personal savior. This dependent need must be processed quickly if patients are to reach a functioning level of autonomy. I consider suicidal fixation, homicidal rage, and obvious proximity to a psychotic break to be the only exceptions to this rule. Even here, the projection of the therapist as "rescuer" carries the risk of a tragic letdown that creates more problems in the long run than it solves. Therapists are often remiss in this regard. Psychiatry tends to exploit dependent personalities (for financial gain?) who expect a parental voice to direct their neuroses in the path of certitude. Such psychiatry neglects the clear difference between assertive reality-testing and authoritarian directives.

More crucial to humor as therapy is creating an atmosphere of trust. The admission of a personal flaw is conducive to such an atmosphere. It can dissolve mountains of resistance that a more austere method tends to buttress. When "bummed out," I'll admit as much if it's about an issue my patients can handle. I remind them that I'm human and have my limits. An authentic encounter requires the mutual recognition of such limits. When a patient can show empathy for a peer, he/she is often on the road to recovery. Especially when an inability to express concern has been a problem.

The patient at the same time needs to be assured that the counselor has enough of a hold on reality to be a worthy model. But this in no sense precludes humor. Indeed, discernable healing occurs when I can elicit a belly laugh while poking fun at myself. The patient learns in the process that he/she is capable of doing the same. The important thing is not to be afraid either to laugh or to be human.

As important and closely related is confronting sociopathy. The sociopath tends to use vulnerability in others as a weapon against them. The "use" of humor may then regress to irony, or pointed sarcasm, in order to be real. I am not above using such sarcasm to counter manipulation, especially when a sociopath is making a naked play for power.

There is a fine line as well between cruelty and direct confrontation. I prefer to sin on the side of kindness. But I am adept at responding in kind to slickly crude evasion. No matter how amusing on the surface, sociopathy masks a callous disregard for the rights of others. It is in this sense childish and deserves a parental response. That response can be as direct as saying, "Knock it off, John" or, "You're pushing me, Mr. Slick." I don't like embarrassing people in front of their peers, but I will do so sharply if the situation requires it. I can go with the flow to a point, but when selfish coercion harms other patients, I react.

DAVID

I remember an adolescent who constantly disrupted "group" with selfish distractions. The silent response of a prolonged stare was in David's case, not enough. A shy peer was in the midst of sharing some painful self-disclosures. David predictably interrupted her difficult words with an insensitive remark. I coldly countered, "Nobody likes a smart ass, David," and returned to the issue at hand. David was stunned. He got surprisingly reflective and a few minutes later added personal insights of his own. The incident was a turning point in our relationship. David knew he was out of bounds. His intent was to destroy the group, and unconsciously, his "family." He was, in fact, seeking the clear limits my retort provided. What his manipulative behavior of course concealed was insecurity. But insecurity does not excuse insensitivity. I thus called David's hand via the use of sarcasm.

Sarcasm is a far cry from humor as therapy. It is rather a "punishment" whose point is the clarification of appropriate limits. My retort merely cleared the air for the possibility of humor's actualization. David came from a rich family and had been spoiled rotten. He'd been showered with material gifts, as a substitute for love and genuine acceptance. Humor, in contrast, is a medium of expression whose felt context is both intimate and authentic. It eludes the formal structures of method (e.g., limit setting) and requires patience to sustain.

Techniques I have found productive include group limericks, role playing, the sharing of cartoons, discussions of short stories, didactic articles, and a collective viewing of movies, video tapes, and records with humorous themes. I have also conducted groups in which I passed out a variety of masks (in proximity to Halloween and April 1) to be worn during quite serious sessions. Looking around the room at a chicken, a clown, a witch, a pig, an elephant, and a therapist in the guise of a gorilla, affects communication. An empathic nod from the gorilla is at once comical and serious. Masks inject a dimension of perception whose specific content is remembered for weeks and months to come. How did it feel saying what you said while wearing the mask? Were you comfortable or uncomfortable? Why? What did your mask represent?

The power of the mask (= *persona* in Greek, from which the word "personality" comes) is as old as antiquity, and as rooted in tradition as Kabuki, Carnival, the Festival of Baal, or Mardis Gras. The mask provides a condoned arena of safety (as if "it's not really me talking") and functions as a kind of truth serum. I do not wish to come across as "flaky" here, but I have seen this experiment trigger too many insights to think it's a frivolous thing to do. Of course being frivolous *is* at certain moments of catharsis the most appropriate way to be. And if nothing else, the exercise provides an often-needed change of pace.

Another technique that enhances the healing power of humor is role-playing. Playing an unfamiliar role can elicit a spontaneous appreciation of humorous contents. A group portrayal of Satir's blamer, scapegoat, egghead, and distracter is illustrative. Why humor occurs when using Satir's technique I can only guess. The answer may lie in drama itself (i.e., playing a role in front of others). There is a ham in all us, I think, in need of affirmation. And drama gives license to playing roles that we fantasize but are afraid to "act out." It may be that role-playing triggers what Freud calls "an economy of expenditure in feeling."[ix] Whatever the reason, Satir's method *works* and is closely linked to an energy that humor taps.

The sharing of cartoons can also trigger humor as therapy. It's best to use an overhead projector so that they can be laughed at by everyone at once. I have amassed a large collection of such cartoons and the simpler their conveyance of common-sense emotions the better.* A Charlie Brown clipping, for example, can inspire identification with feelings of vulnerability in the face of a Lucy-type antagonist (e.g., the hen-pecked spouse). A meaningful discussion often follows.

As small an effort on my part as cutting a cartoon from the paper can do wonders in assuring clients that I care. I have given groups the assignment of collecting cartoons that apply to each person's situation. Cartoons can raise quite personal subjects in a non-threatening way. Cartoons that focus specifically on what it feels like to be a patient are often the most effective.

Bibliotherapy can similarly trigger a flow of humor. A group reading of mini-plays like Woody Allen's *Death Knocks*, or sharing excerpts from Buchwald, Benchley, Twain, etc. (depending always on the awareness of the patients involved) has proven useful. So has Short's *The Gospel According to Peanuts* and myths and legends (e.g., of the Trickster) from other cultures.

A group setting is best for such "experiments" because of the motivation that peer insight inspires. My specific intent is to experience laughing in a spontaneous way. If spontaneous reflection follows, all the better, and it usually does. I am often amazed how a psychological truth in humorous form (as understatement, or in the guise of a cartoon) can trigger an insight in the patient that might not otherwise occur.

Humorous movies that broach serious themes are similar. The

---

* I must admit a debt to Dr. Joel Goodman at this point who gave me the idea of using cartoons at a conference on "Laughter and Play" in Seattle. Joel has been a pioneer in the field and was one of the first to psychologize the relevance of humor to therapeutic concerns. (Cf., The Humor Project, a periodical out of Saratoga, New York that I often distribute to patients in need of some hope.)

antics of Steve Martin, Robin Williams, and Chevy Chase, for example, adeptly put tedious sobriety in proper perspective.* Beyond Camus' absurd conclusion that life is *not worth committing suicide over*, an appreciation of humor is clearly more rewarding. It beats obsessing on the morbidity of the human condition like Reverend Dimmesdale, hands down. Movies are a great elixir because they require no energy to enjoy. They're especially helpful when concentration is an effort. That is, movies afford access to humorous strengths in a disturbed person that reading does not. The same is true of TV programs like *M.A.S.H.*, *All in the Family*, *Hogan's Heroes*, *Gilligan's Island*, *Candid Camera*, *Groucho Marx*, *Northern Exposure*, *Seinfield*, *The Munsters*, *Saturday Night Live*, etc., etc.

Comedy albums are another way to trigger laughter. Although a bit contrived, they've yielded positive results. I have subjected groups in a day care setting to the likes of Bob Newhart, Lily Tomlin, Father Sarducci, and Bill Cosby (again depending on the make-up of the group) without remorse. Humorous lines invariably tickle group members in a way that strikes me as healthy. Avoiding overtly hostile comedians, I encourage group members to react spontaneously, and then to reflect on the feelings they experience in the climax of laughter. "What does it feel like to laugh?" I might ask. Or, "Is laughing comfortable or uncomfortable? How so?" etc. Such questions test the felt impact of humor. They enhance a receptivity to uninhibited urges, and explore the anxiety of reacting to a situation in an unfamiliar way (i.e., humorously).

These groups also bring anhedonia into focus. "Anhedonia" (what Woody Allen almost named *Annie Hall*) is, of course, the inability to experience pleasure. It is an illness whose symptoms go far beyond the realm of psychiatry. Anhedonia afflicts every society, and there are personality types who act out this tendency

---

* Although I like Monty Python, their themes may be too "off the wall" for the emotionally disturbed. A video-tape that has triggered constructive discussions, almost without fail, is Harold and Maud. It of course raises the question of suicide (amongst many others including the enjoyment of life to its fullest) and has proved a tonic to older patients in both an in-patient and out-patient setting.

to deranged extremes. Indeed, I have known anhedonic psychiatrists who were hell-bent on resisting humor until death. Such persons are oblivious to the spontaneity humor elicits. They mourn the death of pleasure in themselves to the point of self-inflicted flagellation. They experience anguish, I think, over what they've angrily denied in themselves. Humor threatens the validity of their angry detachment from the joys of life.

Such detachment is self-defeating. Adept at keeping ambiguity at bay, it leads to withdrawal from as simple a thing as laughing. Let's face it. It's hard not to laugh when an incongruity of life is truly funny. (For example, Gene Wilder and Richard Pryor in jail in a movie.) Indeed, Anhedonia is masochistic and a lot like sleeping on a bed of nails.

I do not mean to make fun of anhedonic people, although fun is a needed prescription. I rather point to laughter as a natural response to humor. Humor is a way of "seeing" that can be learned, just as anhedonia can be unlearned. Humor requires *play* (as opposed to work) to exist, and occurs through practice, and repetition, and learning to laugh. That is, the anhedonic can teach himself to feel comfortable in humor's presence. My fear is that society as a whole has turned anhedonic. We seem compelled by a strict denial of whatever disrupts expedient sobriety. We've evolved a humorless addiction to punishment — in defense of isolation, insulation, and the false security of a glorified past. If that sounds humorless, I'm sorry, and I'm being anhedonic.

Another "trick of the trade" is a French tape of laughter entitled *Eclats de Rire*. That the laughter is in French, of course, doesn't matter. The tape produces silence in a group I think possesses enough tolerance to withstand my "experiment". After three, four, or five minutes of hearing a fellow human chuckle, chortle, snicker, giggle, laugh, and guffaw, I notice a smile, an aborted ha-ha, and the shared camaraderie of group laughs. Our different feelings trigger a lively discussion when the tape ends.

Why does "hearing" laughter affect our emotions? There is no easy answer. But whatever the reasons, laughter's therapeutic role is not trivial. Histrionic types often verbalize the fear of feeling "out of control." Anal-retentive types describe their resistance to a forgotten ability to "relax." Borderline psychotics disclose the perpetual hostility they feel toward being laughed *at*. Exhibitionists try to monopolize the group, and are surprisingly "structured" by brightly timid neurotics. Sociopaths are reminded by peers of their selfish *behavior*. Physically impaired victims of a terminal disease are given undivided attention. Devoutly mute schizophrenics brighten, because of the topic being discussed. Another variable, is the effect of my own sense of humor on the group.

Each therapist must of course adopt methods that suit his/her personality. If a therapist is lacking in humor, he should probably avoid it altogether. Yet I question if such a person should be doing therapy in the first place. Because therapy requires a flexible response to human experience that includes humor. When humor is contrived, it can hinder communication. But excessive sobriety is more harmful still. A humorless therapist reinforces the alienation that gives rise to a need for therapy in the first place.*

There are many ways to convey an openness to humor. My own ways include saying at a clumsy moment: "Go ahead and laugh." Another is to tell a patient when it's appropriate: "You have a good sense of humor." A direct method is simply to laugh. Humor can be mirrored via such phrases as: "There's something funny in that." A phrase that heightens awareness (in anhedonic types especially) is to sincerely ask: "Do you ever feel like laughing?"

---

* A related technique that I haven't mentioned is what I call "Hope Therapy." I have group members fill a page with a series of sentences that begin with the phrase "I hope . . ." I encourage them to hope anything they feel like hoping (from getting along with a boss to peace in the Middle East) without censoring a single hope. We then share what we've hoped. The outcome is invariably hopeful (no small accomplishment in a hospital setting) and opens channels of acceptance that subsequent encounters can affirm. Similar results are triggered by the phrase "I wish . . ." (Although the emotional content of hope is more substantial; and if both techniques are employed, the hope phrase should come at the conclusion of treatment.) Both methods engender a mood of optimism and coincide with humor's actualization.

CHAPTER V

THE JOKE'S ON ME

> "The chief block to therapy is the incapacity of the patient to feel."
> — Rollo May

"It has seemed to us," says Freud, "that the pleasure of wit originates from an economy of expenditure in inhibition, of the comic from an economy of expenditure in thought, and of humor from an economy of expenditure in feeling."[x] Freud has reduced our psychology to an "economy" that obeys mechanical laws like a car responds to a tune-up. Yet his linkage of the pleasure of humor to "feeling" is profound. It suggests that humor is one of our deepest emotions. Beyond being witty or funny looking, humor triggers a release of repressed pain that rational insight misses.

My years as a therapist confirm Freud's conclusion. Humor fosters a spontaneous exchange of feelings at a healthy level of awareness. It tempers volatile feelings, and is a sensitive response to experience too threatening to directly address. Painful problems can be playfully broached without forcing a cognitive response. Humor brings emotional demons to light in a non-threatening way and disarms them of their power. Feelings that are too internalized to be put into words can be "acted out" in the less serious context of humor. A very disturbed patient comes to mind.

JOHN

John was a painfully repressed white male in his late twenties. He was in the middle of a divorce and brittle to the point of losing control. Concrete in his thinking, John responded to remotely personal questions with defensive anger. He had much to be angry about — including the legal loss of his son, an irretrievable marriage, and a lonely childhood. I experienced John as a time bomb about to explode. Humor helped diffuse the intensity of the rage he was feeling. It neither saved his marriage nor worked a miraculous change in behavior. But humor did prompt moments of relaxation amidst tense interaction. I then explored childhood themes that related to the present. These themes included rejection and isolation to the point of odd hallucinations.

The sessions taxed me because of John's fear of rejection. His paranoia heightened his denial of hard realities that had to be faced. I gained John's trust by making fun of myself. I displayed my own ineptness, as it were, to convey the mistake of taking himself so seriously. My ineptness worked. John noticeably relaxed (i.e., bodily) and began to respond in kind. Though slow at putting his feelings into words, he grew less guarded of fears that needed to be vented. On one occasion we shared embarrassing moments. This session strengthened John. He realized that even in the worst of times he could briefly relax.

Humor opened John to pleasure and made him less defensive. I could then raise sensitive questions that John, on his own terms, could accept or reject. The rootedness of humor in feeling is why this happened. John taught me that persons whose main defense is repression are often blind to humor. As Freud notes, they have lost "even the capacity for deriving pleasure from humor when it is presented to them by others."[xi] The role of humor at this point is to free repressed pleasure in connection to painful experience. This is not accomplished through rational analysis. The therapist instead focuses on the enjoyment of relief from pain.

Where repression in an individual is strongest there is a paralysis of the fluidity (humours) that humor requires. Freud attributes this malady to an inhibiting super-ego. If this is true, the therapist should never *force* humor into an encounter. He should instead find ways in which humorous perspectives on guilt-ridden neuroses can be socially approved (e.g., in the context of a group). Humor deepens the emotional content of therapy while creating a relaxed atmosphere in which to explore its meaning. When allowed to flourish, humor is a medium that enhances the honest exchange of feeling.

Through humor the therapist is able to instruct the patient in the art of play. The patient also instructs the therapist. This is true to the degree the patient can playfully respond to humor. Humor thus facilitates an "intersubjective" model of growth that stresses the mutuality of the encounter. It perceives counseling as an art form whose meaning is "felt." Humor transcends the view of therapy as a technical science. Norman O. Brown is instructive. "While psychoanalysis tries to reach the unconscious by extending the conscious," he says:

> " . . . art represents an irruption from the unconscious into the conscious. Art has to assert itself against the hostility of the reality-principle and of reason which is enslaved to the reality-principle. Hence its aim, in Freud's words, is the veiled presentation of deeper truth; hence it wears a mask, a disguise which confuses and fascinates our reason. The mask which seduces us is derived from the play-of the primary process."[xii]

The same can be said of humor in its relation to "the play of the primary process."

As play is a temporary suspension of the laws of reason, humor suspends the critical aspects of therapy that stand in opposition to play. Internalized in the patient as super-ego, humorless severity treats play as its enemy. Such therapy is in keeping with a Cartesian logic. It requires the distance of a thinking subject (doctor) from its object (patient). It thus resists the proximity of play to the unconscious. Conditioned by medical methods in the likeness of cement, the psychiatrist is especially prone to this *in absentia* method. He/she can be an agent of the alienation that this model fosters, and is not therapeutic.

When overly critical, the psychiatrist exaggerates the seriousness of his profession. He encourages in the client an unwarranted subservience to the reality principle. The playful impulse of humor is often dismissed as nonsense and of no meaning. The result is a style of therapy that does justice to neither the complex relation of play to motivation, nor to its role in emotional healing.

WAYNE

I think of a psychiatrist I worked under as a student. I liked Wayne personally but questioned his approach. He'd been in psychoanalysis himself and was well versed in its methods — from both sides of the patient-doctor equation. I know too that he justified his straightlaced detachment in terms of transference. I consider identification as worthy a doctrine, but that's another story. My problem was Wayne's negative impact on severely depressed patients.

I knew the patients in Wayne's group quite well. They dreaded his sessions and, the moment he entered the room, turned dead silent. I value silence and it often precedes an in-depth encounter. It also places responsibility *directly on the patient*. The cause of silence in this case, however, was intimidation. The dialogue Wayne evolved was stilted and unrelaxed. It amounted to what I'd call "the silent treatment." Wayne's approach merely reinforced the fear in group members of the hopelessness of their condition.

If these patients could verbalize their discomfort, Wayne's method may have worked. But they were too emotionally drained even to react. Wayne's method may apply to neurotic and borderline patients. But with this group of patients, it was a disaster. I couldn't blame the failure of the group, as Wayne did, on the patients. The same group responded to another psychiatrist in a hearty way. Adam possessed a delightful sense of humor in sharp contrast to Wayne. He also honed the dialogue these patients needed. The difference in styles was obvious. Adam knew how to play and allowed humor a place in therapy. I'm reminded of the difference between knowing psychoanalytic theory and grasping Freud.

Freud, by the way, knew how to play. He hints at the relevance of play in his discussion of *Wit and Its Relation to the Unconscious*. Wit is present initially, he notes, in the child's earliest experimentation with words and thoughts. "Playing with words and thoughts, motivated by certain pleasures in economy,"[xiii] thus becomes a first stage in the formation of wit, and for our purposes, humor.

"This playing," says Freud, "is stopped by the growing strength of a factor that may be called criticism or reason. The play is then rejected as senseless or as directly absurd, and by virtue of reason it becomes impossible."[xiv] Wit develops as a stubborn protest, according to Freud, in a way that: (1) strives to elude reason; and (2) would substitute an infantile state of mind for adulthood. Freud describes wit's actualization as "the liberation of nonsense."

The same can be said of humor. Humor can free the playful nonsense of energies that contradict the felt repressions of the super-ego. As Freud puts it, "It is really the super-ego which, in humor, speaks kindly words of comfort to the intimidated ego."[xv] Thus the therapist, with the help of transference, can be an agent of self-acceptance. His use of humor casts the internalized fear of authority figures in a kinder light. In the projected guise of super-ego, the therapist helps resolve parental conflicts whose origin lies in childhood. By being sensitive to the playful intent of humor, he replaces the experience of rejection with acceptance.

The relation of humor to feeling here is instructive and *affects* the therapeutic process. For psychic disturbance betrays a disequilibrium of feeling; it reflects a distortion of the natural connection of humor and feeling. An example is the chronically depressed patient. When engaged in humorous encounters he/she often discovers the need to express humor and to enjoy its pleasure. As this occurs the patient displays an equilibrium of feeling and responds more freely to humor when it is offered by others. That is, as patients begin to feel better, their sense of humor improves. A reason is humor's prereflective grasp of emotional well being. It buoys the feelings that the intellect misses. It dispels those demons of repression that inhibit the free flow of emotion as play.

BETH

I recall a fourteen-year-old patient who was so frightened she was unable even to utter her name. Beth was withdrawn to the point of hiding in the closet in a fetal position. I tried to sense her vulnerability without being impatient or patronizing. This meant repeating my name and my wish to be her friend. Often we simply sat in silence as I assured Beth it was "all right if she didn't feel like talking . . . sometimes there's just nothing to say." Beth began to acknowledge my presence and slowly granted me access to her inner world.

My approach included empathic encouragement and non-threatening humor. Soft-spoken understatement of Beth's silence proved especially helpful. For example, "We can't go on meeting like this" or, "Would you consider talking about the weather?" I recall her first courageous reply. "I like your voice," she said. "Thank you," I answered, "I like yours too." As time went on cracks began to appear in her wall of shyness. One day her eyes sparkled when I responded with laughter at her attempt at making another patient laugh. That moment was a turning point in both our relationship and Beth's marked improvement.

As her story unfolded I understood why. Beth's parents were talkative, self-righteous, and controlling. Their goal was "protecting her" from the evils of the world. They could see no difference between what they thought was best for Beth and Beth's discovery of the same for herself. Beth in turn perceived their values as beyond reproach. She saw herself as a receptacle of their demands. To question their demands would mean to look at the reasons for her parents' need to keep Beth submissive. This step was too threatening to take because it would rock the family boat. Beth felt confused and indecisive to the same degree that they had made her an object of manipulation. She was thus robbed of her autonomy. Her parents did this in a way that was humorless and smug.

Beth's discovery of humor was important. It was a means of combating the innocence her parents projected. They perceived the spontaneity of humor as a threat. It was a chink in the armor of their stubborn rigidity. Humor after all was honest. It might lead to anger and the admission of marital problems. In the course of therapy, Beth described hell as "a place where no one is allowed to laugh." Family implications were obvious.

Humor became a key to unlocking repressed urges that Beth was afraid to admit even to herself. Her fear was the motive in the seriousness of her parents' disapproval. Their insistence on perfection was obsessive. It was rooted for both in resentment and deep-seated conflicts in their relationship. Their repression of these conflicts had been projected onto Beth in deceptive ways. In repressing their own feelings, they were oppressing Beth. They could deny the intensity of their feelings only as long as she submitted to their denial of any problems. That meant yielding and being blindly obedient to authoritarian commands.

Beth was as hooked on dependency as her parents were hooked on keeping her dependent. Playing victim was preferable to the anguish of disrupting her security. It was easier to "give in" than fight an unwinnable battle of independence. Especially when confrontation would be a source of pain to her parents. Beth read her urge to express such feelings as proof of her inadequacy as a daughter. She was trapped in a no-win situation as the focus and rope of a parental tug of war. Eventually the rope snapped in an explosion of guilt and angry withdrawal.

Humor helped Beth realize that she was not restricted to her family role. She was living a tragi-comedy whose lead role she didn't have to play. She could even choose not to take the scenario seriously. Viewing her situation with humor enabled Beth to broach the anger she felt for having been given such a lousy part. She discovered the weak link in her parents' armor to be a void of humor. Thus humor made them human and was a means of self-assertion. It proved valuable in confronting her parents during a family session. They opened up considerably when Beth called them "an American Gothic version of the Coneheads."

The sharing that followed was gut level, genuine, and in some ways angry. Because of humor, the session was much less threatening, both to Beth and to her parents. Beth's mother admitted needing "to work on our sense of humor." What Beth had discovered was the power in humor to arouse honest communication. It was her point of entry to a new world of independence. Beth personified for me the truth of Freud's insistence on the kinship of humor and feeling.

Another way to *unblock* feelings with humor is what Frankl calls paradoxical intent. He believes that grasping the humor of a fear makes it disappear. "By exaggerating the phobia," he adds, "one is able to cure it."[xvi] Frankl thinks that taking the phobia too seriously only strengthens its grasp. His method is to conquer the seriousness of the phobia by expanding its nonsense. Despite its irrational form, the phobia is present for good reasons, and requires a penetration that vents its *raison d'etre*. Exploring a fear thus includes embellishing its laughable content. This means exposing the phobia, umbilical cord and all. The patient literally laughs the phobia away, and grasps through humor how ridiculous his phobia is. The paradox lies in treating the phobia in an opposite way than expected.

JAN

Jan, for example, was frightened to death of crowds. Jan's problems included a volatile fixation on the approval of her mother. Her fear of being judged would surface in crowds in the likeness of

Chicken Little. She was also a compulsive talker. She was at present in a panic at the thought of going to the grocery store alone.

"What do you have against grocery stores?" I asked. "It's not grocery stores," she answered. "It's the people. I'm afraid of what they might be thinking." Instead of telling Jan that her fear was ridiculous, I agreed. I quickly rattled off the frightening aspects of buying groceries. I asked Jan to add scarier items to the list (which she quickly did). The longer the list got the more ridiculous her phobia became. "Plus," I concluded, "you might not be able to open your purse when it came time to pay the cashier." Jan laughed, and pointing to her purse, added, "My fingers might get stuck on the strap." The next day Jan successfully conquered the travails of grocery shopping.

VICTOR FRANKL

Frankl relates a dramatic example of the same thing. His patient was a surgeon who trembled uncontrollably whenever a superior entered the operating room. Frankl's suggestion was to exaggerate the nervous condition "as much and as loudly as possible to show what a good trembler he was."[xvii] In the midst of an operation the surgeon followed Frankl's advice. Remarkably the trembling stopped, never to occur again. Frankl's tongue-in-cheek method fully embraced the client's compulsion and for this reason was paradoxical. That is, by taking the neurosis seriously enough not to take its form seriously, its frightening aspect was overcome. Instead of resisting the neurotic impulse, Frankl carried the neurosis to its most absurd conclusion. His response was ingenious and instinctive. But why did it work?

Frankl resisted obsessing on the obvious symptom of trembling hands. His more telling aim was to exorcise the neurosis completely. The crucial questions he asked were, why did the client need to make a fool of himself in the first place? Why did he feel so intimidated in front of authority figures? What protest, perhaps against paternal aggression, was being feebly enacted?

Whatever the causes of his reaction, and they are not difficult to imagine, Frankl's paradoxical intent delved below the surface of obsessive fears to their unconscious source.

Like the phobia, paradox has no apparent basis in reason. Unlike the phobia, it finds pleasure (rather than fear) in its contradiction of reason. Reason after all is relative and merely the normal way of doing things. What is reasonable to a Zulu tribesman would be entirely unreasonable to a Western executive. And vice versa. The phobia in a similar way is unreasonable. It has an unconscious logic and amounts to a contradiction of what's normally expected.

What the phobic misses is that being unreasonable can be fun. This is the genius of paradox. It recognizes *as it were* the unreasonable need in the phobic to liberate nonsense. The absurdity of the phobia can then be relativized in the light of *all* absurdity. Thus paradox fosters a process of healing whose initial stage is unrelated to critical analysis.

Such a process can be encouraged with the aim of later reflection. But reflection is secondary to its felt impact. To the extent neurotic fears are irrational, their influence is contradicted in the act of embracing their nonsense. The role of humor, in relation to paradox, is to inflate the phobia to absurd proportions. The client can then laugh *at* the phobia and even embrace it. As Allport puts it: "The neurotic who learns to laugh at himself may be on the way to self-management, perhaps to cure."[xviii] Paradoxically, he is able to take the humor of his situation seriously by being less serious about his phobia.

A paradoxical problem is the tension between the need to get hostile feelings *out*, and their effect on sensitive peers. I am more exposed still to hostile behavior, and it requires an outlet. A way to cope, I've discovered, is to embellish the absurdity of a situation from my own perspective. In a theatrical way, for example, I can "go crazy" in front of the group. This method especially disarms adolescents, and it particularly helped George.

GEORGE

George had managed once again to disrupt the group at just the wrong time. I put my hands to my head and went berserk. "All right, George, you win! I can't take it any more! Why me, Lord? Go ahead! Take my job! Take what it's taken me ten years to learn how to do! It doesn't matter. Here, take my coat! (handing him my coat) And my shirt! Do you want my shirt? Take it all. And the group too! Take the group. It doesn't matter George. It doesn't matter! And the rest of you, go ahead! Let George monopolize the group. It doesn't matter. Who cares? My mother told me I should have sold insurance! It doesn't matter. Who needs a therapist when you've got Cheech and Chong?" Without letting George get a word in edgewise, I abruptly left the room. The group suspected I was kidding, but wasn't entirely sure. I gave them enough time to process their response in hopes I could sway the group in a responsible direction. When I returned to the room I got a paradoxical shock in return.

I found the group being quietly led by its most disruptive member. George was wearing my coat, stroking his chin, and insightfully nodding. I sat in my chair with tongue in cheek and listened to a meaningful group encounter. What my paradoxical approach accomplished I'm not sure. But I'm certain it accomplished something. The opposites it juxtaposed included: an affirmation of George amidst his negative effect on peers; the communication of my own anger while responding to the needs of the group; a humorous context for, and integration of, what was George's *misuse* of humor; and a test of the level of trust on which the group could build.

ANGELA

I think of a chronically depressed woman in her early fifties. Angela was the most stoic person I've ever met. Her body language was rigid, closed, and totally controlled. She sat in the same chair for hours on end with her feet planted squarely on the floor. Her arms were outstretched and motionless. Angela was heavyset, and burdened with a weight of worry beyond her years. She had dark, piercing eyes that scorned any intruder. Angela's presence was to say the least, intense. She was preoccupied with fiercely morbid thoughts. She verbalized rage at her husband's "confusion of his penis with a gun." She required careful treatment, and conveyed every irritation with a deadly stare of defiance.

Dodging the hate in Angela's eyes, I quietly asked her what she was thinking about. Her answer as always was short and curt. She said without flinching, "Suicide." Angela was *serious* about death. Her answer was *absolutely honest* and demanded *no nonsense*. Her deliberate statements in group were: "I always tell the truth," and "Why do you ask?" I respected Angela's need for privacy, and that she was very suicidal. She internalized *every angry feeling* and was unable to handle or calmly express this emotion. The only way she could convey her rage was through ironic negation.

Her last defense against overwhelming despair was ironic detachment. Her irony was an indirect way of letting off steam. All of the above filtered my response to Angela's blunt answer to what she was thinking of doing.

I shared the insight of Camus that life was "not worth committing suicide over." Angela immediately brightened. My comment tapped Angela's keen sense of irony. It visibly popped the bubble of her fixation on suicide. It verified her right to be feeling the way she was feeling; and that I too was not content with pat answers. I couldn't talk Angela out of her belief that life was meaningless and not worth living. Yet I could remind her that suicide doesn't necessarily follow. Why commit suicide if life doesn't deserve the gesture?

Such is the stuff of irony. My paradoxical approach left Angela's ironic negation of life intact. Irony in fact was her desperate way of surviving life. Denying her this defense was a risk I wasn't willing to take. For this reason, Kierkegaard's decision to move beyond irony to humor didn't apply to Angela. She didn't commit suicide. I hope she's alive, and I wonder how Angela is doing now. I hope she is less bitter and is being kinder to herself.

When suicide or decompensation is the alternative, an ironic defense is best left alone. Irony functions as a detached expression of uncomfortably angry emotions. It vents hostility from a distance, about emotions, intensely felt, without taking the risk of vulnerability. What irony avoids is personal involvement in the moment. Such involvement for Angela was unbearable. It required an expenditure of energy that was painful, and couldn't be spared. She avoided direct emotion via impersonal detachment. What could not be embraced could be stung and numbed from a distance.

Angela was not overtly antagonistic. She was instead hostile toward the intrusion of her carefully guarded space. That space, over an extended period of time, could be cautiously entered. Just as Angela's irony could in time be humored. The immediate task, however, was to evolve Angela beyond her suicidal fixation. This meant being frank and shrewdly supportive.

HERBERT

I remember a patient who gave Job a run for his money. His life read like a sequel to "The Attack of the Killer Tomatoes!" It's safe to say that if Martians ever landed, it would be in Herbert's backyard. His first wife had died in an accident at work. He'd lost a house in a fire caused by lightning. His second wife ran away with a marshmallow salesman; and I'm only scratching the surface. But what Herbert had kept alive against impossible odds was his sense of humor. Humor may have been all that Herbert had left to keep alive.

Afraid of sounding cruel, Herbert's woeful descriptions of his life, at times left me in stitches. He was at heart a comedian and gifted in humorous insight. He used humor as a needed defense. It enabled him to couch tragic experience in a light that purged the pain of its articulation. Herbert's disarming understatements were spoken with a flat affect. For example: "I would describe myself as a failure." Such statements were true. But spoken in the tone of a Bob Newhart, they were also funny.

Herbert's gift was putting personal failure in perspective. He helped *me* in a similar way. In the light of Herbert's failures, my own failures seemed inconsequential. If Herbert could see the humor in taking life too seriously, so could I. His insight is needed medicine for a society as obsessed with "winning" as our own. For every winner (taker) there is a loser (giver) who fails (gives in). If winning weren't taken so seriously, could we finally free ourselves of the fear and doublebinds of "failing"?

Failure *after all* is the redeeming feature of *being human*. To grasp this truth is a sign of maturity, because nobody's perfect. And to obsess on perfection, without enjoying our follies is absurd. Humor intuits the courage to laugh in the midst of the absurd. Its gift is its graceful acceptance of imperfection. The climax of such acceptance is heartfelt laughter.

BOBBY

One of the most delightful persons I have ever met was a Vietnam veteran who'd been paralyzed in combat from the waist down. When I met Lt. Muller he was touring the country giving speeches from a wheelchair. Bobby had been to hell and back by way of Hamburger Hill. But what I remember beyond his speeches and personal conversation was his laugh. His laugh was the most distinctive I've ever heard. The tone of his laugh was neither hostile nor demonic. It was rather hearty, infectious and loving. Bobby intimately knew the fragile brevity of life in the face of death. He also knew pain. What this knowledge had taught him, and what his sense of humor conveyed, was love. Or rather, the love Bobby displayed had resolved every contradiction including the finality of death. Bobby was unconditionally accepting of the many human beings he had touched.

RICH

I think of an eccentric colleague named Rich. Rich knows as much about Freud as I know about the migration patterns of ducks. Yet he applies wit and humor to therapy in a masterful way. Consider his success with a very paranoid patient. The patient was defiant, and accused Rich of being a witch doctor. He also thought that Rich "and the rest of you devils are spraying me with evil spirits." Needless to say, his patient was *resistant to treatment*.

The next day Rich entered his room with a can of spray deodorant. Rich began chanting, dancing, and dousing the room with Right® Guard. The patient asked him what he was doing. Rich responded, "I'm a witch doctor and I'm spraying your room with evil spirits." Rich claims the moment was a breakthrough in their relationship. I take Rich's word for it. If Freud were alive, he would have smiled.

ANDREA

I remember a client who had the recurring dream of being chased by a bear. The nightmare upset Andrea to the point of an obsession and was a frequent cause of insomnia. The bear turned out to be her father, who curiously was quite hairy. This connection became clear in the course of exploring incestuous themes. As we unraveled Andrea's mixed feelings toward "daddy" the dream stopped.

I pointed this out to Andrea. "It reminds me," I said, "of two campers being chased by a bear. One of them shouts, 'Go faster or we won't be able to outrun the bear.' 'Who's trying to outrun the bear,' answered the other camper. "I'm trying to outrun you." Andrea realized that the bear she was outrunning was herself. Or rather, it was the projection of her own anger. Her anger was too frightening to face directly. So she had cloaked it in a nightmare in a frightening form. Her real anger was at having to feel afraid of her father. Andrea discovered that she no longer needed to protect *him* from *her* in the guise of a bear. She could directly face the good and the bad that her father was. Sometimes a bear is just a bear. And sometimes a joke about a bear is just a joke about a bear.

CHAPTER VI

THE LAST DUCK TO GIGGLE

> "The serious hero focuses events, forces issues, and causes catastrophes; but the fool by his mere presence dissolves events, evades issues, and throws doubt on the finality of fact."
>
> — Enid Welsford

A way of making humor conscious that I haven't mentioned is my use of limericks in what I call "poetry therapy." I conduct these sessions in as relaxed a manner as possible. I use various kinds of poetry to elicit feelings that might not surface in normal discussion. My playful intent in the case of limericks is what Freud terms "the liberation of nonsense." I've been surprised by the amount of repressed sexuality that limericks spontaneously free. Subconscious wishes are vented through limericks without being condemned or experienced as guilt.

A sense of humor, via a sensitivity to repressed feelings, is what allows this to happen. Limericks after all are only limericks. They have a non-critical aim that is very simple. They teach us to have fun with words while letting language rhyme itself. They trigger fantasies we would fain to utter in normal conversation, because friends would think us crazy. Such fantasizing is essential to emotional well being. Fantasy is a buffer, and a way of surviving the serious world of work and obligations. To "daydream" in fact is a natural and healthy outlet. It is a way of relaxing and even being "lazy" — which for a workaholic is a *chore in itself*. And when not done to extremes, it should be encouraged.

There is a world of difference too between having fantasies and acting them out. This distinction is crucial and should be clearly noted when fantasies are a cause of neurotic guilt. As imagination enhances a more fluid encounter with the real world, dreaming dissolves the contradictions of conscious experience via the *recreation* of an image. The irony is that we are so intent on *facing reality* that we cut ourselves off from its *unconscious* face. We don't remember our dreams; we reduce the soul of wit to second-class status; we refuse to allow fantasies to reach fruition. The alternative to fantasizing is to be stilted. Similarly, limericks free libidinal projections in the light of play.

The following limerick, by a staid and inhibited English teacher, makes my point:

> There once was a lady from Trent
> Whose mind was heaven bent
> But her body liked fun
> So She played in the sun
> Now she runs a brothel in Kent.

Susan's limerick worked as an instrument of healing. It put guilt-ridden thoughts in a humorous form that could be socially approved and momentarily transcended. What was an unconscious expression of sexual needs, shackled by a rigidly Puritanical upbringing, could be brought to uncensored light in the form of a limerick. As important, the limerick brought pleasure to Susan's peers.

I have discovered group poetry to be a great source of encouragement to depressed patients. The optimum number for such a group is six to eight members. I've done poetry therapy with much larger numbers, but size inhibits the exploration of each person's story. Human themes can then be personally discussed, and sharply honed. For instance, death, tragedy, joy, love.

Poetry's access to deeply personal feelings is striking. It opens private vistas of reality that we are barely able to put in words. As important is poetry's concreteness and clarity of expression. It links us directly to an image that can then trigger self-discovery. Such self-discovery may or may not be humorous. In keeping with Aristotle's sense of happiness, humor is "an activity of the soul in accord with virtue." That is, humor is a natural outgrowth of integrity. It is intrinsic to "the process" and cannot be forced. Of the three types of poetry I employ — free verse, haiku, and limericks — only limericks are directly aimed at creating laughter.

I begin by noting my lay interest in poetry. A reading of poems by Stevens, Frost, Eliot, Ferlinghetti, Cummings, etc. follows. (I avoid Sylvia Plath because of the anxiety her tragic end can trigger.) I approach them in no sense as a critic; I rather unravel feelings that an image evokes. A reading of Stevens' "The Emperor of Ice Cream," for example, can elicit responses normal dialogue ignores. The poem reads:

> Call the roller of big cigars,
> The muscular one, and bid him whip
> In kitchen cups concupiscent curds.
> Let the wenches dawdle in such dress
> As they are used to wear, and let the boys
> Bring flowers in last month's newspapers.
> Let be be finale of seem.
> The only emperor is the emperor of ice-cream.
> Take from the dresser of deal.
> Lacking the three glass knobs, that sheet
> On which she embroidered fantails once
> And spread it so as to cover her face.
> If her horny feet protrude, they come
> To show how cold she is, and dumb.
> Let the lamp affix it, beam.
> The only emperor is the emperor of ice-cream.

I focus on Stevens' mood when writing the poem. Was he happy, sad, pensive, etc.? The aim of such questions is identification; their "correct" answer doesn't matter *as long as members are grappling with the poem's imagery in a personal way.* Images allow us direct access to the poet as a person. What, for example, does Stevens mean by "the emperor of ice-cream"? One person answers, "The shortness of life. It tastes good for awhile and then it's gone." "That seems to be part of what he's saying. Any other ideas?" "I think it's the shallowness of values that melt away to nothing." "How so?" "The line 'let be be finale of seem' says it all. He's telling us that the way things seem to be is the way they really are. And right now they ain't so hot. You got genteel ladies and macho politicians, but we all go out the same hole in the end." "That is an interpretation. What else comes to mind?" etc.

My own respect for Stevens is considerable. I regard him, for aesthetic reasons, as without peer amongst American poets (apart from T.S. Eliot having been reared in St. Louis). He is truly the poet of the imagination. Yet I refrain from imposing my own sensitivities on the group. The last thing persons in crisis need is a lecture on the "pathetic fallacy." I may answer off the wall remarks with a humorous aside (e.g., "Surely you jest."); but I avoid playing artistic judge. Therapy is the simplest medium of art and therefore the most human. Its aim is to affirm what is uniquely human in each person regardless of his/her intelligence. This includes relieving anxieties whose frequent cause is felt inadequacy. Again, the purpose of poetry therapy is to provide an outlet for repressed feelings that might not otherwise be expressed. Thus poets like Cummings and Ferlinghetti inspire more comments. A reason is that they require minimal abstraction and tap the emotions directly. They are a primer as well for group experiments in free verse.

Consider the following poem:

> In Just-
> spring when the world is mud-
> luscious the little
> lame balloonman

>   whistles far and wee
>
>   and eddieandbill come
>   running from marbles and
>   piracies and it's
>   spring
>
>   when the world is puddle-wonderful
>   the queer
>   old balloonman whistles
>   far and wee
>   and bettyandisbel come dancing
>
>   from hop-scotch and jump-rope and
>   it's
>   spring
>   and
>   the
>   goat-footed
>
>   balloonMan whistles
>   far
>   and wee

 Cumming's poem defies every rule of syntax. It is free verse at its freest without regard for grammar, spelling, capital letters, etc. Its whimsical style evokes lively and varied reactions. Some patients think it's bittersweet and cynical. Others think it a celebration of innocence, rebirth, and humanity (Just-Man). Specific interpretations, however, are inconsequential to my intent. What the poem frees in group members is nonsensical phrases that come directly from the unconscious. It thus serves as a creative catalyst of individual concerns. The poem prompts ambiguous thoughts and feelings to surface without fear of reprisal from me.

 With chalk in hand, I ask the group for a list of free floating images. They are to do this without regard for meaning or making sense. It's helpful if the therapist adds to the list to dispel the fear that such word-pictures are "crazy." The images are sometimes loaded with pre-conscious insight. Each person then writes a poem from the list. I point out that there is no wrong way to associate whatever phrases his/her mind chooses to put together. The poems are then read aloud. Different configurations of the same phrases are often striking but should not be dwelt upon.

The next step is individual. Each person is to fill a piece of paper with uncensored images from himself. "Anything goes," I say, "and the crazier the better." Each group member then connects his images in "whatever way seems right to you." The less the therapist inserts himself here the better. But with a reticent group he/she must sometimes be a catalyst. My discovery has been that the primary process speaks for itself. Patients often marvel at what their poems reveal. Especially when they let phrases complete themselves without censoring their content. A group process evolves as I encourage peers to react to, and empathize with, the feeling a poem connotes. I'll ask the group, for example, to identify images that are striking and to give reasons why. Each person interprets the poem and its relevance to his/her situation. Humor often spontaneously occurs, and can then be affirmed; but it is rarely my conscious intent.

Besides compiling a collection of fairly decent poems, my free verse approach to therapy usually accomplishes the following: (1) the patient discovers the creative power of his/her imagination; (2) he/she receives affirmation and insight from the group; (3) he/she feels less threatened by inner voices that he may be too embarrassed to share with others; (4) he/she is reminded that there is a poetic world and a practical world and that poetry is a way of expressing the former in an appropriate context; (5) the therapist is afforded a direct glimpse of unconscious conflicts that would otherwise remain hidden; (6) the patient learns that he/she can "handle" (i.e., put in concrete form) disjointed thoughts by uniting them in a poem; (7) the patient learns to value his/her feelings and the right to express them; (8) the image becomes a symbol that can be clarified and evolved in later sessions; (9) what is labeled "loose association" is given credence in the context of poetry; and (10) dissociative feelings are "concretized" and vented.

As a primer to the above, I sometimes follow a conceptual framework. An example is having each member complete the following lines: (1) sometimes I feel so angry . . .; (2) sometimes I feel so sad . . .; and (3) sometimes I feel so happy . . . The sequence here is important. Because the last series of responses leaves the patient with a more hopeful feeling about his/her situation. This exercise requires a full session and though not purely poetic, can point the client to alternative moods of awareness. It is important that the patient learns to integrate such moods. Thus the tendency to obsess on a single feeling to the exclusion of others (e.g., self-pity) is diffused. Also, emotions that the patient has trouble expressing can be brought to conscious awareness. This emotion often is anger. Anger normally must be vented before the pain it protects can be put in words. Always, the emphasis is on free expression without regard for logic or "making sense."

It is important too that the individual "dramatize" the mood being expressed. This helps him claim and exorcise feelings he would normally repress. When verbalizing anger, for example, he/she might be loudly vociferous, crumple his paper, and throw it across the room. If such anger is present it does no good to structure therapy in a way that denies its intensity. Otherwise the anger remains, and it carries the risk of regression to a self-consuming rage. It's also helpful to give the poem a title. This prompts discussion as well as giving the client a sense of closure on the content of the poem. And the poem should be dated for the same reason.

A group member gave me permission to print several of her poems. Nanci suffers from juvenile diabetes. Besides facing blindness and the loss of circulation, she's had to contend with considerable personal trauma. I've been impressed with her courage and the increasing maturity of her insights. She claims the group has "helped me more than you'll ever know. During my worst depression the only thing that kept me sane was sitting down and writing a poem. It freed me, and for awhile I forgot my problems." The following is some *free verse* she has written:

Disregarded
she escapes the tangled sheets;
hands tremble for hot coffee
and a seat
calculated for loneliness.

People
avoiding touch
with passing glances
make discrete plans
for their
day.

Bedlam
begins;
she moves . . .
a child
on the first day of
school.

Tears -
rain blurs the window
as she longs for the soft
of her cat's fur.

Time, ever slowly
fills with words
carefully chosen to disguise,
carelessly spoken to reveal.

Finally
doors close
ending a day -
drifting . . .
drifting toward
oblivion.

                              N.M.

Satiated pink bedroom walls
        crib secrets,
palisade the frightened child.

Solemn prayers:
little hands clasped together
beg for undisturbed sleep.

Find the soiled teddy bear
limp from insides spilling
with each embrace.
Crawl underneath warm blankets
        . . . and wait.
Animality enters through the bedroom door,
penetrates the child's secure domain,
bruises picture-book fantasies of tender moments,
maternal eyes
peer through white lace curtains,
unresponsive to pillowed screams
within.

A silent dawn of apologies
and promises never kept.

Hide in playground swings.
Pushing hard, let wind dry tears,
blow thoughts toward white-grey morning clouds

moving slowly through the blue
of another
day.

                                                N.M.

—

Ride high
on a snowflake
melting
as I
land.
Running frolics leave prints
in the snow -
afternoon sun melts the day
and
no one knows
I
played.

                                                N.M.

I follow free verse with a change of pace *à la* the limerick. Limericks are great in this regard, and they diffuse the intensity that free verse often heightens. Limericks prompt a celebration of nonsense as comic relief.

The group first creates a limerick together. I ask for a person's name and two words that rhyme (e.g., Fred, bed, head). I write these in the appropriate place on a blackboard and ask for two more words that rhyme (e.g., zoo, Kalamazoo). Group members do the rest. For example:

> There once was a bum named *Fred*
> Who spent all his days in *bed*.
> He slept in a *zoo*
> Near *Kalamazoo*
> Where a bear bit off his *head*.

Such limericks reveal more psychology than meets the eye; but too close an inspection limits the spontaneity they require. I thus spend no time on interpretation and rather encourage the catharsis of laughter. Group members often use the name of peers. This develops camaraderie. Writing limericks also sharpens the awareness that therapy need not be deadly serious. Frivolous example are as follows:

>There once was a man named Sam
>Whose appearance was that of a lamb.
>One day he awoke;
>Take note what he spoke.
>"I'd rather be me than a ham."
>
>———
>
>I once knew a talented pig
>Who wore a magnificent wig.
>Though dressed quite bizarre,
>Folks thought him a star.
>Now in movies he dances the jig.
>
>———
>
>There once was a king from France
>Who horrified the girls with a glance.
>His demeanor was charming,
>His manners disarming,
>But he had a great hole in his pants.

I've noted too that the rhythm of limericks helps structure psychotic patients. My simpler aim, however, is to have fun. And fun is no small feat amidst the trauma of being hospitalized for a neurotic breakdown.

My poetic method concludes with *Haiku*. Haiku's healing agents include intuitive clarity, a simple rhythm (5-7-5) and form, and an identification with nature. Haiku naturally evolves a sense of oneness with "the image." This sense transcends rational analysis. My discovery is that the image stands in immediate relation to *awareness as dimension* and a breakdown of rational defenses (ego-diffusion). That is, the patient can express himself as a "camera of being" without resorting to the defenses of an autonomous ego that normalcy requires. Consider the following haiku written by a nearly catatonic patient:

> The wave loudly lands,
> Sprays the shore with salty smells,
> Painted shells recline.
>
> D.S.

After reading her poem, I noticed in Diane a brighter face and a more composed sense of self. Her stoic demeanor softened and she was able to identify with the poetry of her peers. A reason for this change, I think, is haiku's profoundly simple aim. That is, by picturing a *seasonal* scene from nature *in the present tense* the patient glimpses a pre-rational unity that is essentially complete. The regular rhythm of haiku gives a sense of continuity. Reflectively detached, haiku calms, and gives closure to conflict that limericks heighten.

What the limerick celebrates as contradiction haiku softens and mends in the light of contentment. Humor lies somewhere in between with properties in common with both. Whereas the limerick laughs *at* and *outwardly* without regard for integration, haiku inwardly resolves via its oneness with nature. Its imagery *rests* in the human relation of perception to the totality of creation; it brings to light the intuition of existence that transcends what we experience as contradiction. More simply, haiku completes and resolves what the limerick begins. Humor is adaptive and blends with both poetic forms.

See examples of haiku my patients have written:

> Pinetrees fluffed with snow,
> Tumbling down to pat the ground
> winter whitely dreams.
>
> D.K.

> Mother blows like March
> > turning my grand piano
> > > any way she chooses.
>
> A.T.
>
> Footprints in the sand
> > following west toward the sun
> > > erased by the sea.
>
> A.T.

Laughter occasionally spiced *all* of the poetry groups. I would describe it in the case of free verse as cathartic, in limericks as haughty, and in haiku as soft and gentle. A reason such laughter occurred is poetry's immediate grasp of primary emotions. And different types of poetry prompted differing styles of therapy. It follows that humor's form is intimately linked to feeling.

SARAH

I think of a patient who was diagnosed by her analyst as a "borderline personality disorder." Sarah was admitted to our program after repetitively carving skin from her arm with a knife. She was above average in intelligence and very stubborn. Her history included a lesbian relationship with a former professor. Their breakup had catalyzed self-destructive behavior, including attempted suicides, and a rage she conveyed with a darting stare. Sarah was suspicious of the simplest of questions, and for several days merely looked at the floor. She milked laborious periods of silence for every ounce of power they were worth. She was husky, tall, big-boned, and muscular, and projected her body as a weapon.

I sensed in our encounters that Sarah's temper might explode in either a homicidal or suicidal direction. Her female peers were frightened to death. I can think of no patient who *demanded* as much attention and gave so little in return. Her intimidating stare conveyed primitive projections of her parents onto everyone in the room. I was thus surprised when after a month of laborious reality-testing, Sarah gave me eight haiku "as material for your book." They were neatly typed and intended as "a gift" I value:

(1)

The snow falls softly
Gusty winds turn your nose cold
Leafless trees are white.

(2)

Cold winds breeze through town
Old men walk the empty streets
Clouds cover the sun.

(3)

Flowers gasp for air
The heat rises from the streets
Sweat drips from your chin.

(4)

The hot sun appears
The rainbow shines in the sky
A misty rain falls.

(5)

A bird sings gently
The sun rises with great joy
children play outside.

(6)

Leaves fall to the ground
Where the grass dies to our eyes
Clouds cover the sun.

(7)

Hail pounds the hard earth
Heavy rains fall from the sky
Leaves swirl from the trees.

(8)

The sun brightly shines
Where the flowers bloom with glee
The morning dew dries.

Sarah's poems are sensitive and hopeful. As the level of trust between us grew, I found Sarah to be in possession of quite playful traits.

The point of this chapter is that what poetry and humor share in common is play. Both in fact are *rooted in play*. As Huizinga writes in *Homo Ludens*: "Play we have found is so innate to poetry, and every form of poetic utterance so intimately bound up with the structure of play, that the bond between them is indissoluble."[xix] Huizinga makes the same point in terms of laughter, folly, wit, jest, jokes, the comic, sport, language, myth, ritual, music, art, and even philosophy and law. Play is as intrinsic to consciousness as what Groucho Marx means when he absurdly asks: "Why a duck?"

I am fond of ducks, by the way, and find them amusing. I've discovered conducting group sessions at a local duck pond to be therapeutic. There's something funny about the way ducks quack, waddle, splash, and flap their wings. I think ducks teach us something in how they play. Some people, including psychiatrists, are less adept at play than ducks. Their funny antics remind us as well that it's okay to be "the last duck to giggle." This is especially true if an ugly duckling is really a swan.

CHAPTER VII

YOU'RE KILLING ME

> "As the crackling of thorns, under a pot, so is the laughter of the fool."
>
> — Solomon

SOREN AND FRITZ

Few thinkers have grasped the essence of humor as deeply as Soren Kierkegaard. It is crucial to both his thought and the formation of "the self I am meant to be." Without a sense of humor, he would have likely committed suicide or gone permanently insane. The Groucho Marx of philosophy, Kierkegaard's humor is prolific.

The key to Kierkegaard's humor lies in moving beyond ironic negation. He thinks irony is inferior to a life stance that is at root affirmative, and this is what distinguishes him from Friedrich Nietzsche. Even so, Kierkegaard is painfully conscious of the relation of irony and humor. He fears his own affinity for the ironical stance and sides with humor out of necessity. He sees humor is the best medicine for his despair, and for the illness that will cause his early death. After seriously considering suicide, Kierkegaard writes this in his diary:

> When an ironist laughs at the whimsicalities and witticisms of a humorist, he is like the vulture tearing away at Prometheus' liver, for the humorist's whimsicalities are not capricious little darlings but the sons of pain, and with every

one of them goes a little piece of his innermost entrails, and it is the emaciated ironist who needs the humorist's desperate depth.* His laughter is often the grin of death.[xx]

There is in Kierkegaard, as in Freud, an appreciation of the intimate connection of humor and feeling. This connection thwarts the rejection of feeling that typifies irony. Because humor grasps the problem of pain more deeply. Humor can juxtapose both the meaning and absurdity of human existence, and does not succumb to irony's resentment. As Kierkegaard puts it: "The ironical position is essentially *nil admirari*; but irony, when it slays itself, has disdained everything with humor, itself included."[xxi]

Insights relevant to therapy here are several. They in some ways temper Kierkegaard's "sense" of humor. There are times, for example, when a client is unable to move beyond irony. Irony becomes a weapon of last resort. Couched in a posture that spurns vulnerability, its clear message is "stay away." Irony attacks what is perceived as a threat to its emotional isolation. Such a defense, if unhealthy in the long run, can thwart insights too threatening to embrace.

Nietzsche similarly writes: "Objection, evasion, distrust and irony are signs of health. Everything absolute belongs to pathology." Nietzsche is in the exact position of the patient whose irony is a defense of last resort. Nietzsche is right that any rigidity (e.g., reaction formation or an obsessive-compulsive disorder) too inflexible to change, regresses to sickness. Rigidity destroys "life" and mistakes for "either/or" what is really a process. What Nietzsche's irony misses, however, is precisely Kierkegaard's point. Namely,

---

* Kierkegaard's allusion to "the humorist's desperate depth" in the face of death reminds me of Freud's affirmation of Eros. Freud's will to live included writing an essay on gallows humor while in the process of dying from cancer of the jaw. Many people, as Freud notes, do not possess "even the capacity for deriving pleasure from humor when it is presented to them by others." (Character and Culture, p. 268.) I like Freud's "sense" of humor being a gift; and to the extent a surprising percentage of the patients I see are anhedonic, his reference to the "capacity for deriving pleasure from humor" hits the nail on the head.

life consists of stages of growth in which humor is more vital than evasion, objection, and distrust. Kierkegaard's penetration of irony coincides with Hyers' insight that "Humor moves from playful innocence through truth and justice to humility and compassion."

Kierkegaard's point of view, however, does not always "work" in therapy. Humor opens *the subject* to a pattern of health that certain types of pathology cannot attain. And the decision in therapy to penetrate an ironic defense should be tempered by the patient's need to construct this defense in the first place. This is especially true if a patient is paranoid. His/her use of irony is somewhat justified. Irony is often a foil against a world that confirms paranoia. (Fanon, for example, defines paranoia as a rational response to an irrational situation.) Irony can be a desperate attempt to battle what a patient feels as overwhelming fears. It accomplishes what May calls the intent of the "schizoid personality." Irony defends the psyche from emotional depletion, and the "spiritual vacuum" of love reduced to will.

The use of irony in a political context applies to therapy. When aimed at curing social ills — for example, Lenny Bruce, Dick Gregory, George Carlin, Richard Pryor, and Chris Rock[xxii] — irony taps a rich vein of activism. Such irony should be respected, no matter how profane its polemic. It possesses integrity and the strength of its conviction. Political irony is the cutting edge of a more humane social order. But irony differs from humor in a crucial way. Humor has no agenda beyond the joy of its actualization — for example Bill Cosby, Gene Wilder, Dana Carvey. Political irony, in contrast, is directly aimed at changing society. What I mean by irony is akin to what Freud calls hostile wit.

DICK AND BILL

Dick Gregory and Bill Cosby are examples. Gregory's so-called "black humor" was politically intended. In search of social justice, it was a dagger aimed at an oppressive system. Gregory was a court jester for the underdog. He pricked the middle class conscience in a way that power politics could not. Gregory's following amongst WASP youth during the late sixties and early seventies was remarkable. He ridiculed racism to the delight of students whose parents were its cause. The laughter Gregory inspired was ironically induced. He made an ethical point of what it meant to be in Dick Gregory's skin. His wit was double-edged and a tongue-in-cheek exaggeration of resentment in himself. He put the evils of bigotry in absurd perspective.

"I know niggers who hate onions," I remember Gregory saying at Emory in 1969 with his bodyguards on stage. His ironical remark was doubly aimed at white racism amidst the ironies of black experience. The audience felt its ethical sting while laughing at the absurd image of hating an onion. The tone of Gregory's tongue was softened by his curious blend of anger and ethical concern.

What moved the audience was personal conscience and knowing the difference between right and wrong. Gregory's ideals are clear in his later activism via fasts, demonstrations, and treks across the country on behalf of the homeless. The audience was swayed by Gregory's identification with oppression in a personal way. We can't help but laugh when he intones, "I never met a Klansman in a dark alley I didn't like." Gregory's use of political irony was direct and pointed. His purpose was *and is* to make injustice conscious.

Bill Cosby, in contrast, is less of a politician and more of a psychologist. His style is softer but every bit as effective. Playfully open, what Cosby shares is himself; he projects and elicits warmth in a believable way. We say to ourselves, "I like this man." The reason, I think, is simple: Cosby touches the common chord of our humanity whose origin lies in childhood. His exaggeration of babycrib phobias tickles the funnybone of our own experience. We can't help identifying with "ice cream" and the omnipresence of "Fat Albert." Cosby's genius lies in being able to see the world through the eyes of the child. He reminds us of the child in ourselves, that each one of us is a child grown up. That may be what humor is. Humor captures in the present the continuity of feeling that links us to childhood.

For Cosby, too, the medium is the message. What Gregory politicizes, Cosby conveys. Racial themes in Cosby are clearly present; but they are *indirectly* raised. It's not "healthy" to be a racist because we deny ourselves the humor Cosby allows us to enjoy. His gift of gab is peppered with disarming doses of compassion. Not as abrupt as Gregory, his humor penetrates the bigotry of white and black alike. Cosby reminds us of the maturity in wisdom of being childlike. The aim of humor in therapy is the same. I thus consider Cosby a humorist and Gregory a political ironist.

Honest therapy, especially in an interracial setting, should not summarily dismiss political irony. Labeling such irony adolescent (which by its rebellion against structures of power it necessarily is) only begs the question. It may say more about the psychiatrist's socioeconomic status than the client's condition. And social defiance for ethical reasons has a justification of its own. The very practice of therapy, of course, by virtue of its fruition in time and culture has political roots.

I do not mean to suggest that therapy be politicized or that irony's antisocial stance be naively affirmed. But therapy is a context for appraising the client's ability to handle the strain that being a "rebel" entails. The tendency of social activists to mistake "inner" reality for "outer" reality (e.g., projecting father onto "the man") is no less dangerous than the opposite tendency of psychology. Both viewpoints are in their way justified. They must be fairly balanced if therapy is to keep its integrity.

Every therapeutic response that is in some sense "corrective" includes an ethical judgement; because even a hint of social adjustment reflects the morality of the group that the therapist as "super-ego" represents. The ethical question that always remains, after all, is what values are we "adjusting" the patient to? We ought at least be open to exploring the worth of those values in a universal light. The courageous task embraced by Freud (before being forced to flee Hitler's Vienna) is instructive. He directly contradicted "adjustment" to a de-ranged *projection of value* by the herd. Social adjustment, therefore, may be a dangerous value *to value.*

My simple point is that we all make judgements of value; and value judgements are an historical given that clearly affect the therapeutic process. The sensitive therapist should at least be conscious of the ethical assumptions in the models that he/she employs. Future generations will likely view *us* in the same light that we view nineteenth century asylums. What I pray we don't lose is the humanitarian impulse that has broadly guided our tradition. History reminds us of the importance of this impulse. And we are no more immune to its abuse than was Germany a generation ago.

We are the fortuitous heirs of a humanist tradition (as opposed to the despotic fideism of so many societies) that has likewise formed psychology. In cross-fertilization with the growth of democratic institutions, valuing "the individual" made the practice of therapy possible. To be blind to these influences is to be reactionary, in the same sense that Tory resistance to the American Revolution was reactionary. Thus political irony deserves an occasional hearing. Its ethical form especially is historically important.

Consider the tendency of humor to surface in those who feel the brunt of oppression. Humor helps relieve the irony suffering breeds. It is an outlet for emotions whose experiential cause is the unfairness of life to the rejected segments of society. When shared with the community at large humor can evolve the honesty that social progress requires. I believe humor to be one of our lasting contributions to culture (amidst many dubious ones) in the world historical sense of the term. We are such a dissimilar blend of cultures that we have needed humor to survive our contradictions. Each wave of immigrants, including the Poles, made its humorous contribution to the polity at large. As Belden Lane puts it:

> "The Holy Fool breaks down structures of *political order*; when everyone else is silent before the royal naked-

ness, he alone laughs at the king. He or she may also break down structures of *language*, speaking a new Jabberwocky or nonsense, using words in the most inappropriate way. The Holy Fool breaks down structures of *social propriety* by acting ridiculous and childlike."[xxiii]

The fool's words, as Shakespeare proves, are of course spiced with considerable doses of irony.

Sensitivity to irony's ethical side, however, isn't the main business of therapy. Therapy requires an honest exchange of feeling in an atmosphere of trust. Irony, as a rationalization of less conscious levels of awareness, often thwarts such feeling. It triggers humor as a corrective to what is *wrong* in ourselves. The key here is humor's softer focus. It coaxes gently without polarizing, in a way that irony's bite does not.

Like poetry or ballet, prompting humor is an art form. Humor's actualization requires a grasp of intuitive perceptions. Among these is a sense of the appropriate moment to be inappropriate. The artistry of humor lies in its conspicuous defiance of conventional norms of behavior — without paying the price of social rejection. If taken literally, the more serious implications of humor's defiance would be seen as a threat. Due in part to humor's access to emotions that engender affection, however, it broaches normally taboo subjects with minimal resistance.

A reason for this is humor's sensitivity to feelings that repel subservience to the reality-principle. No matter how ingrained the dictates of the super-ego, there exists in everyone a wish to defy "authority." This is especially true when social pressure is perceived as an enemy of needed pleasure. Humor arouses unspoken permission to deviate from the norm. It gives poetic license to contradict the co-optation of personal autonomy by normative restrictions. Humor's artistic task is to *make fun* of the sobriety in modern society that the rational nature of work requires. Its happy medium is play.

By the same token there is good humor, bad humor and attempts at humor that miserably fail. The beauty of humor as an art form is its acceptance of failure as an ingredient in the mix of humor's creation. Also, being *quick-witted* is not the same as being *humorous*. Wit is more pointed in response to an insult and tends to raise the horns of ironic spite. Wit is a conceptual approximation of what humor intuits.* What humor intuits is hope in the midst of despair.

This is not to say that humor is naive or Pollyanna. Far from it. Humor just refuses to let failure have the last word. It takes failure seriously, but no more so, than the absurdity of taking failure with more seriousness than it truly deserves. Such seriousness "blocks" the relativity of a particular failure in the light of *all* failure in the history of human beings.

In an ideal sense, humor and laughter are interdependent expressions of the same process. They can thus occur simultaneously. The two are not identical, however, and a conceptual refinement of their differences is needed. As often as they are confused, these differences cannot be overstated. This is especially true for a culture in as desperate need of humor as our own. Laughter, for example, can be biologically defined. It is the "spontaneous contraction of 15 facial muscles stimulated by electrical impulses of increasing strength concurrent with sporadic breathing." Humor in turn cannot. It thwarts every attempt of nominalism (i.e., naming and defining "things") to explain away humor's subjective source. Laughter too can be devoid of any humorous insight. It can be a cruel enemy of the feeling that humor shares and protects.

Such laughter is pernicious in its intent. It reminds me of Goethe's remark that men show their character in what they think laughable. Cruel laughter conceals an unresolved hostility that thwarts the honest exchange of emotion. Its tendency is to mistake irony and/or ridicule for humor. This tendency betrays a deep-seated cynicism that is at root nihilistic. Laughter (and its manipulation) then becomes a weapon that vents anger at the futility

---

* and is a stone's throw away from the Old World's fixation on the insult.

of life. Its calculated goal is the belittlement of hope that humor enhances.*

Laughter that is truly related to humor, in contrast, relativizes even death. It was Origen who likened being wise to the child who can frolic and play beside his parents' coffin. In simple terms, the laugh of humor is an outward celebration of the inward realization of unexpected joy. Such joy, at subliminal levels, includes a felt transcendence of mortality. Its laugh is grounded in the conviction that, despite a lot of evidence to the contrary, hope endures and the universe is good. Thus the laughter humor raises comes directly from the soul. It occurs where the humorous bond of feeling and sound express a communion whose pleasure is felt as fun. Healthy laughter is akin to what Homer calls "the deathless laughter of the gods."

At root, humor is the feeling that discerns pleasure in the possibility of unconditional love. Its concealed hope is integration as love beyond hate's disintegration. Such love is conceivable only after chaos and its destructive influence has been emotionally digested. The humor that love forms is entirely in accord here with life-affirming laughter. But it does not require expression as sound to exist. It follows that humor cannot exist without a silent sense of the possibility of love.

That human kindness is the deepest core of our lives is the enduring conviction of humor's courage to be. Being in touch with humor thus amounts to possessing faith in love. This raises in the imagination the connection of faith and paradox in some of the existentialists. There is a love that exists without paradox as a *condition* of acceptance; and there is a love that embraces the paradox of love that is *unconditional*. The difference between the two is that conditional love is more easily threatened by a disequilibrium of emotion. Conditional love abstracts itself from any negative feeling that requires a "leap of faith" to overcome.

---

* Cf. Jean Wright's comment in the context of pastoral counseling that: "Just as a man/woman may be diagnosed as sexually dysfunctional when unable to experience orgasm, so one can be diagnosed as affectively dysfunctional when unable to experience the pleasure of laughing and/or smiling."

The *condition* of such love is a denial of feeling in the light of painful experience. Conditional love disconnects itself from any anxiety that threatens rational control. It can tolerate neither contradictions nor the paradoxical possibility of their resolution. It thus denies the pain in others in order to deny the pain in itself. To let language speak itself, the condition of conditional love in the unconditional face of paradox, *is conditional.*

Unconditional love, on the other hand, accepts pain in the light of its paradoxical liberation. The paradox of pain comes to awareness via the conjecture that life could have been created without pain; and for this reason is unfair. To live in the paradox means to understand pain (from the inside-out as it were), and then to affirm life in the light of its painful conclusion. That is, the paradox of pain that unconditional love is nurtured by, contains an ultimate cure. And all contradictions of thought (as a reversal of reason by way of "the absurd") are *felt* as being absolutely resolved.

To possess a sense of humor, in turn, is to be in touch with the possibility of unconditional love. Humor's grasp of pain includes a deeper understanding of life's incongruities than merely being able to laugh at oneself, although laughing at oneself is central to it. A deep sense of humor implies acceptance of the imagery of unconscious despair (and the imagination's resolution of such despair through love) as an ultimate concern that is essentially religious.

What I mean by religious is in no sense parochial. Without demanding that God appear on a white horse *deus ex machina*, the religious antennae continues to penetrate important levels of awareness. The good theologians do this in a way that is superior to both second-level psychology and the heavy-handed tactics of empirical investigation. Their insights are important to therapy, and we have much more to learn from the likes of Moltmann, Buber, Tillich, Unamuno, Marcel, Maritain, Eliade, etc.

The above discussion relates to therapy in several ways. It reminds us, first, that a sense of humor is more than the myopic woolgathering of a deluded subject. Humor is rather *inborn*; it is an attribute unique to our species that may be redemptive. Humor's power is vitalized via contact with the "real" world. Humor at the same time softens the world's bite. From a soft-spoken stance of inwardness, when our tendency is to be lost in externals, humor reminds us of our depth. When our tendency is withdrawal, humor awakens us to active engagement with our milieu.

Humor's curious interplay of *inner* and *outer* encourages receptivity to the world from within. Such receptivity is linked to the same vein of intimacy that therapy requires. It includes ignoring pretense and letting a dialogue of trust evolve.

Also, an appreciation of humor can be learned. Although callously neglected, humor is an intuitive intelligence that can be nourished and improved. This occurs through contact with significant others whose sense of humor is more fully developed. When grounded in self-acceptance, humor is a medium of growth and visceral acceptance. At this level, acceptance and the sharing of acceptance (i.e., love) are the optimum possibilities of human awareness. Love interacts with humor and enhances the likelihood of humor's realization.

Humor is a fluid in the body of love (as feeling) whose configuration in the self's receptivity to humor is *the sense* of humor. When grounded in mutual acceptance, humor heightens sensitivity to inner conflicts. It is crucial to a personal encounter with the emotional trauma that therapy bridges. Dissociation from the external world, for example, can be humorously tempered and spiced with practical doses of reality. Humor's role is to soothe the pain of confrontation with the balm of self-acceptance.

It follows that laughter, as one expression of humor, may be entirely in accord with humor. Laughter can also be the clanging harangue of humor's opposite. When disconnected from love (as hostility or scorn), it is so out of touch with humor that we cringe in dismay. Such laughter signals a death of feeling amidst the paradox of pain. It harms the hope that unconditional love in the face of pain seeks to strengthen.

The survival of civility depends on distinguishing laughter that is informed by humor and laughter that is not. When in tune with their difference, the therapist can be an agent of healing. His/her humorous intent is echoed in the wit of Maurice Chevalier. Chevalier was asked on his birthday how it felt to be eighty. He answered: "It beats the alternative." Humor beats the alternative.

CHAPTER VIII

THE CONTORTIONS OF A GUFFAW

> "A man may love a paradox without losing either his wit or his honesty."
>
> — Emerson

A paradox is an apparent contradiction that isn't really a contradiction. It is a first cousin of humor and has cross-cultural implications. In opposite ways, paradox "informs" both Eastern mysticism and Western existentialism. Both kinds of paradox apply to therapy and uniquely shape the contortions of a guffaw.

In Buddhism, paradox is inwardly resolved through intuition. Paradox reacquaints us with a depth that the mystery of the earth opens. Without recourse to reason, it intuits that resolution precedes contradiction. Before "yes" and "no" there is the unity of One. There is no sense figuring things out because reality can only be grasped from within. Amidst apparent contradictions, is the inscrutable sound of "one hand clapping." Humor comes to awareness in Zen via an intuitive acceptance of paradox in direct relation to nature. Humor dwells within the immanent center of Yin and Yang as the completion of "bliss" or *satori*.

Paradox is central to the "mystical communion" of Mother Church in the history of the West as well. But in religious existentialism, after Luther, Descartes, and Pascal, the opposite is true. Paradox turns transcendent, and humor is stretched to a conception of "the absurd." What happened? What events "disciplined" Western history in such a paradoxical direction? The answer is complexly simple. The pitch of the absurd in the West increases as reason is removed from the "sphere" of the earth. The absurd occurs as thought detaches man from nature through astronomy, science, and rational perception.

The paradoxical difference between East and West lies in the West's differentiation of the rational function since Plato. This combines with the Hebrew faith in a personal God of history. The burden the West carries is its progressive fusion of time with objective reason. As reason is lifted from intuition, thought negates emotion and requires a paradox (Kierkegaard) that is "transcendental." Paradox in the East, in contrast, is intuitive and "immanental."

My dilemma as a therapist is which paradox practically fits the patient. If a patient's background is nominally religious, there is no need to explore Kierkegaardian tensions. Such tensions may be subliminally present, however, and eventually require the "leap of faith" of a Western solution. Otherwise, the simpler instruction of Zen — to dissolve the complexities of thought (=anxiety) with intuition — applies. Paradoxical humor in the East is softer focused. It enjoys humor as it comes, in harmonious relation to the simplicity of "being". Its humor is centered in an immediate sense of pleasure that remarkably calms neurotic symptoms. Western paradox also seeks pleasure, but because of moral complexities, delays its gratification.

JONAH

A 32-year-old patient named Jonah better conveys what I'm trying to say. Jonah came from a strict, Pietistic family. He was devoutly religious and very bright. He was also a "true believer," and his first instinct, for complexly moral reasons, was to resist pleasure. Jonah's psyche was a battleground of fierce beliefs and absolutes. He'd imbibed the "prophetic" tradition (Isaiah, Jeremiah,

Ezekiel, Daniel) from his parents and felt "called" to be an agent of societal healing to a sacrificial degree. His staunchly ethical father was a Protestant pastor who, beyond coincidence, was named Amos. Jonah's righteous conscience challenged my ethics and rattled my brain. Considering the condition of society, I was hard-pressed for a reason to doubt the validity of Jonah's calling.

Jonah censored spontaneous feelings, and spurned "the carnal nature" of pleasure. His stoic theology included a rigid belief in the Trinity and "original sin." Yet, Jonah was radically progressive in his political views, and he'd spent years of community service in the inner city. I paid Jonah the compliment of letting him know he had as much to teach me, as me him. He asked me to read a typed journal of spiritual reflections that echoed the *Diary of a Country Priest* by Bernanos. His paragraphs were filled with a remarkable compassion for the poor. His words pitted "the reality principle" against a self-imposed duty "to do God's will."

Jonah worked with the underprivileged every day, and was good at what he did. His commitment to social justice was a religious way of rebelling against his conservative father. Jonah was torn between his Biblical faith in a loving God, and the pain in the lives of his "down and out" clients. His psychological problem was being unable to enjoy life, without first negating "amoral" joy for moral reasons. Jonah's fixation on Judeo-Christian guilt required a more complex and decisive solution than Buddhist intuition. He required a paradoxical response that could untangle the knots in the Western roots of his religious tradition. So I let our therapy turn in a "Kierkegaardian" direction.

Know I respected Jonah's integrity, passion, commitment, and keen mind. My only concern was how much moral conflict he could emotionally stand. I didn't want him to end up with a bad back and ulcers at the age of forty. I had no right to tamper with Jonah's theology if it weakened his faith, and thus would weaken him. Indeed, Jonah's belief in a supra-historical God who conquers ALL contradictions (justifiably grounded in Barthian and Neo-orthodox thought) was a vital key to improving his mental health. My role as a counselor was to create an outlet for Jonah's ethico-religious tensions. Jonah was intense, dialectical, and "deadly serious." He was as tight as a rubber band about to snap; he needed to unwind and learn to relax. I discovered that using paradoxical thoughts spiced with humor was a practical way to get Jonah to "lighten up."

During a tense session, I mentioned Goethe's insight that: "the devil never laughs." When Jonah used the word "irony" in a grave moment, I noted how ironical it was "that Lou Gehrig died of Lou Gehrig's disease." I listened carefully, and made it clear that poking fun at Jonah's seriousness, never excluded my respect for him. I remembered Elie Wiesel's wisdom: "The best answer to fanaticism is a sense of humor." After a tedious period of existential digging, I discovered buried in Jonah, a rich sense of humor.

There are "religious types" who require the assurance of an absolute beyond feeling, that transcends thought, and in a paradoxical sense is emotional. Jonah was such a person and I was sensitive to his evangelical tradition. He was surprised when I called Kierkegaard "the Groucho Marx of theology" and a discussion followed on the closeness of humor and faith in Kierkegaard's thought. Kierkegaard's grasp of passion, decisiveness, and The Paradox of Christianity (i.e., of God in human form) opened channels of feeling in Jonah that included laughter. A helpful tool was a collection of Kierkegaard's paradoxical parables. They triggered a movement in Jonah's thinking and dented his depression. At the end of four consecutive sessions, I handed Jonah a parable on a note card, and asked him to ponder it during the week. These are the parables that Jonah read in sequence:

> *It happened that a fire broke out backstage in a theater. The clown came out to inform the public. They thought it was just a jest and applauded. He repeated his warning, they shouted even louder. So I think the world will come to an end amid general applause from all the wits, who believe it is a joke.*[xxiv]

It is related of a peasant who came (barefooted) to the Capital, and had so much money that he could buy himself a pair of shoes and stockings and still had enough left over to get drunk on — it is related that as he was trying in his drunken state to find his way home, he lay down in the middle of the highway and fell asleep. Then along came a wagon, and the driver shouted at him to move or he would run over his legs. Then the drunken peasant awoke, looked at his legs, and since by reason of the shoes and stockings he didn't recognize them, he said to the driver, "Drive on, they are not my legs."[xxv]

As it befell Parmeniscus in the legend, who in the cave of Trophonius lost the power to laugh, but got it back again on the island of Delos, at the sight of the shapeless block exhibited there as the goddess Leto, so it has befallen me. When I was young, I forgot how to laugh in the cave of Trophonius; when I was older, I opened my eyes and beheld reality, at which I began to laugh, and since then I have not stopped laughing. I saw that the meaning of life was to secure a livelihood, and that its goal was to attain a high position; that love's rich dream was marriage with an heiress; that friendship's blessing was help in official difficulties; that wisdom was what the majority assumed it to be; that enthusiasm consisted in making a speech; that it was courage to risk the loss of ten dollars; that kindness consisted in saying, "You are welcome" at the dinner table; that piety consisted in going to communion once a year. This I saw, and I laughed.[xxvi]

Something wonderful has happened to me. I was caught up into the seventh heaven. There sat all the gods in assembly. By special grace I was granted the privilege of making a wish. "Wilt that you," said Mercury, "have youth or beauty or power or a long life or the most beautiful maiden or any of the other glories we have in the chest? Choose, but only one thing." For the moment I was at a loss. Then I addressed myself to the gods as follows: "Most honorable contemporaries, I choose this one thing, that I may always have the laugh on my side." Not one of the gods said a word; on the contrary, they all began to laugh. From that I concluded that my wish was granted, and found that the gods knew how to express themselves with taste; for it would hardly have been suitable for them to have answered gravely: "Thy wish is granted."[xxvii]

We are a far cry from a mystical resolution of paradox via Buddhist intuition. Kierkegaard's parables are humorous and paradoxical in a Western way. They have a moral and an individual meaning that is also earthy. The voice of a clown, a drunk, an ironical cynic, and a humorist in heaven, triggered key insights in Jonah, and were a touchstone of communication. Paradoxical thinking (e.g., Kierkegaard, Frankl, Maslow, May) especially helps patients like Jonah with a severely strict super-ego.

An example of Eastern paradox is the Japanese folk tale of "The Boy and the Duck." I've used the story in groups and found it to be very therapeutic. Consider its softer meaning:

THE BOY AND THE DUCK

Today I will tell you the story of something that happened shortly after Ooka was appointed Chief Judge in Edo. He wanted to familiarize himself with all the cases being tried, and as he read through the records, one case caught his attention. It was very recent.

The offender was a young fish peddler called Yoshimatsu. On his way home the previous evening he walked along the moat surrounding the Shogun's castle. It was filled with water and a flock of wild ducks nested on the bank. At this time of year it was forbidden to kill a single duck — under pain of death. The boy was very hungry after spending the whole day rushing around the town, and seeing the birds the vision of a tasty roast rose before his eyes. As it was already dark he thought nobody would see him. He picked up a stone, and threw it at one of the ducks as it flew up from the rushes. His aim was good and the bird fell to the ground. Yoshimatsu rushed to get it but just as he picked it up he was suddenly surrounded on all sides by guards. They bound him and took him to court, taking the dead duck with them.

When Ooka finished reading the report, he summoned the judge whose seal was on the document.

An elderly man appeared. His hair was already going gray and his step had long lost its youthful briskness. His face was expressionless and revealed nothing. He was in the formal dress of a Lower Judge of Yoriki. There were twenty-five such judges at the court of the South Town. They learned their duties from early youth, sitting at a respectful distance from the judge during court proceedings. Though the salary was low, their power was great. Like other Banner Knights they carried two swords in their belts and could use them to punish on the spot anyone who displeased them. Until Ooka took up office, the fate of all offenders lay in their hands and their decisions were never questioned.

Ooka showed the documents to the judge and asked him, "What sentence is hanging over this boy?"

"Death," was the brief answer. Without any more ado the judge prepared to leave, presuming the discussion had ended, but Ooka gestured for him to stay.

"How old is the lad?" he asked.

"12."

"Why does a child like that sell fish?"

"His father died when he was eight," the Yoriki answered reluctantly. "He has a mother and two sisters."

"What about his mother?"

"She is ill and has been confined to bed for several years."

"So the boy provides for her as well as the two sisters?"

"Yes, Your Honor," the judge confirmed in a voice that showed surprise Ooka was making so much fuss about such a simple case.

"Is he to be sentenced to death?" Ooka asked.

"Yes, that is the law," the judge replied coldly.

"Have the guards bring the boy here," Ooka ordered.

"As you wish, Your Honor," replied the Yoriki, bowing.

Before long the young offender knelt stiffly before Ooka on the white sand covering the courtyard.

"Is it true you have killed a duck?" Ooka asked him.

"Yes, Your Honor."

"If that is so, then I want to see the duck, bring it here," he told one of the court assistants waiting nearby. Two of them got up immediately to do as Ooka ordered. Soon the duck was lying in front of the judge.

"Is this it?" asked Ooka, lifting the duck up so that the accused could see it.

"Yes, it is," the boy answered.

"Are you sure it is the same one?"

"Yes."

Ooka passed his hand over the duck's neck and said, "But it is still warm!"

The boy looked up in surprise as if he could not believe his ears.

"See for yourself!" Ooka told the boy and handed him the duck. "Now take it, and find somebody who will help you to bring it back to life."

Yoshimatsu was quick to see what the judge had in mind. He took the duck and ran as fast as his legs would carry him to Anjin poultry market. Here he found a live duck which looked exactly the same, and took it back to the court.

"There, you see, you have managed to bring it back to life." Ooka smiled. "The matter is settled. Go back to your mother and sisters and may you all live happily for a long time to come."

When the boy told his family what had happened to him, in her joy his mother sat up in bed for the first time in years. From that moment her sickness gradually improved and before long she was quite well again.

A mystical-intuitive approach is very helpful with neurotic symptoms, and resolves conflict at the level of simple feeling. It nurtures in a maternal way without regard for the contradictory impulses of a rational dialectic. The paradox it uncovers opens our awareness of being a channel of imagination's play. The humor of such paradox is self-contained amusement that we probably first experienced in the womb.

Contentment and the communication of contentment are a basic aim of therapy and very important. The therapist's first goal is to calm desperate fears, and get the patient in touch with a "secure center" that is grounded in hope. The therapist is an agent of the felt assurance that the patient is accepted from *without* and from *within*. Therapy tempers volatile thoughts via a relaxed penetration of anxiety in the first person. Relaxation in the therapist cues a relaxed response in the patient that often triggers self-acceptance.

Self-acceptance can arise from either an Eastern or Western sense of paradox. All I care about as a therapist is if my patient gets better and the paradox works. To repeat the point of this chapter, both forms of paradox are a medium of the healing power of humor, play, and laughter. They have prompted me, in the ennui of sleepless nights, to support Pat Paulson for President.

CHAPTER IX

DID FREUD SNICKER?

> "Wit marries ideas lying wide apart by a sudden jerk of the understanding."
> — E. F. Whipple

Freud sheds important light on humor in *Wit and Its Relation to the Unconscious*. This is true despite his reduction of wit to inhibition and humor to emotion. Inhibition and emotion are *obviously linked* to both. More helpful is Freud's distinction between tendentious wit and harmless wit. Harmless wit approaches what I mean by humor, and is especially instructive, as is the book as a whole. What follows is a summary of the book with relevant comments.

Freud begins by noting the importance of this much-neglected subject. "Our philosophical inquiries," he says, "have not awarded to wit the important role that it plays in our mental life. One can recount only a small number of thinkers who have penetrated at all deeply into the problem of wit."[xxviii] The same can be said of humor. Like wit, humor is a "connection which promises to furnish psychological insight into a sphere which, though remote, will nevertheless be of considerable value to the other spheres."[xxix] Freud's subsequent classification of twenty wit techniques is laborious and of less interest than the jokes he employs as examples.

Most noteworthy is the technique of nonsense. "Sense in nonsense," says Freud, "transforms nonsense into wit."[xxx] That is, wit occurs when an illogical movement of thought yields a logical insight. Our tendency is to disregard nonsense because it doesn't *make sense* or conform to logic. We forget that nonsense has a logic of its own and are then surprised.

Under the heading of "displacement," Freud offers a memorable joke: "Two Jews meet near a bathing establishment. 'Have you taken a bath lately?' asked one. 'How's that?' replies the other. 'Is one missing?'"[xxxi] Freud hints at the earthiness of wit. "We demand no patent of nobility for our examples," he writes, "nor do we make inquiries about their origin. The only qualifications we require are that they should make us laugh and serve our theoretical interest."[xxxii] Laughter precedes analysis, in other words, and becomes a source of insight. Freud's study is reductionistic, meticulous and overly schematic. Even so, his jokes are worth repeating, and will be listed under the technique they represent.

    a. "condensation with substitutive formation"
    e.g., "In that part of the Reisebilder entitled 'Die Bader Von Lucca,' Heine introduces the precious character, Hirsch-Hyacinth, the Hamburg lottery agent and curer of coins, who boasting to the poet of his relationship with the rich Baron Rothchild, ends thus: 'And as true as I pray that the Lord may grant me all good things, I sat next to Solomon Rothchild, who treated me just as if I were his equal, quite famillionaire.'"[xxxiii]

    b. "condensation with modification and substitution"
    e.g., "... a well-known witty jest of Mr. H., who remarked about a character in public life that he had a 'great future behind him.'"[xxxiv]

    c. "wit formed by word-division"
    "A witticism of this sort was utilized by an Italian lady to avenge a tactless remark made to her by the first Napoleon. Pointing to her compatriots at a court ball, he said: 'Tutti gli Italiani danzano si male' (All Italians dance so badly). To

which she quickly replied: 'Non tutti, ma buona parte.' (Not all, but a great many.) —*Buona parte.* [xxxv] Buonaparte

d. "manifold application of the same material"
e.g., "How goes it?" asked the blind man of the lame one. "As you see," replied the lame one to the blind."[xxxvi]

e. "double meaning and play on words"
e.g., "Discharge thyself of our company, Pistol" (Henry IV, Act II).[xxxvii]

e.g., "A physician, leaving the sick-bed of a wife, whose husband accompanied him, exclaimed doubtfully: 'I do not like her looks.' 'I have not liked her looks for a long time,' was the quick rejoinder of the husband."[xxxviii]

f. "ambiguity"
"A good example to illustrate this is the story told of a wealthy but elderly gentleman who showed his devotion to a young actress by many lavish gifts. Being a respectable girl, she took the first opportunity to discourage his attentions by telling him that her heart was already given to another man. 'I never aspired as high as that,' was his polite answer."[xxxix]

g. "the tendency to economy" (observation)
"Condensation thus remains as the chief category. A compressing or—to be more exact—an economic tendency controls all these techniques.... It may be true that every technique of wit shows the tendency to economize in expression, but the relationship is not reversible. Not every economy in expression or every brevity is witty on that account."[xl]

h. "puns"
e.g., "Professor Cromwell says that Rome in exchanging her religion changed Jupiter to Jew Peter."[xli]

i. "displacement"

e.g., "Two Jews meet near a bathing establishment. 'Have you taken a bath?' asked one. 'How's that?' replies the other. 'Is one missing?'"[xlii]

j. "nonsense as a technical means"

—"sense in nonsense transforms nonsense into wit."[xliii]

e.g., "Itzig has been declared fit for service in the artillery. He was clearly an intelligent lad, but intractable and without interest in the service. One of his officers who was friendly disposed to him, took him aside and said: 'Itzig, you're no use to us. I'll give you a piece of advice: buy yourself a cannon and make yourself independent.'"[xliv]

e.g., "Never to be born would be the best thing for mortal men. But," adds the philosophical comment in Flegende Blatter, "this happens to scarcely one person in a hundred thousand."[xlv]

k. "sophistic faulty thinking"

e.g., "The agent is defending the girl he has proposed against the attacks of her prospective fiancé. 'The mother-in-law does not suit me,' the latter remarks. 'She is a crabby, foolish person.' 'That's true,' replies the agent, 'but you are not going to marry the mother-in-law but the daughter.' 'Yes, but she is no longer young, and she is not pretty either.' 'That's nothing: if she is not young or pretty, you can trust her all the more. 'But she hasn't much money.' 'Why talk of money: Are you going to marry money? You want a wife, don't you?' But she is a hunchback.' 'Well, what of that? Do you expect her to have no blemishes at all?'"[xlvi]

l. "automatic errors of thought"
e.g., "On being introduced to his prospective bride, the suitor was rather unpleasantly surprised, and drawing aside the marriage agent, he reproachfully whispered to him: 'Why have you brought me here? She is ugly and old. She squints, has bad teeth and bleary eyes.' 'You can talk louder,' interrupted the agent. 'She is deaf, too.'"[xlvii]

m. "unification"
e.g., "Human life is divided into two halves; during the first, one looks forward to the second, and during the second, one looks backward to the first."[xlviii]

n. "representation through the opposite"
"Frederick the Great heard of a Silesian clergyman who had the reputation of communicating with spirits. He sent for him and received him with the following question: 'Can you call up ghosts?' 'At your pleasure, Your Majesty,' replied the clergyman, 'but they won't come.'"[xlix]

o. "outdoing-wit"
e.g., "A Jew noticed remnants of food on the beard of another. 'I can tell you what you ate yesterday,' he remarked. 'Well, let's hear it,' said the other. 'Beans,' said the first one. 'You are wrong,' responded the other. 'I had beans the day before yesterday.'"[l]

p. "indirect expression with allusion"
e.g., "By undertaking a series of risky schemes, two not very scrupulous business men had succeeded in amassing an enormous fortune and were now intent on forcing their way into good society. Among other things, they thought it advisable to have their portraits painted by the most prominent and most expensive painters in the city, men whose works were considered masterpieces. The costly pictures were

exhibited for the first time at a great evening gathering, and the hosts themselves led the most prominent connoisseur and art critic to the wall of the salon on which both portraits were hanging side by side, in order to elicit from him a favorable criticism. He examined the portraits for a long time, then shook his head as if he were missing something. At length, he pointed to the bare space between the pictures, and asked: 'And where is the savior?'"[li]

q. "omission"
e.g., "A wife is like an umbrella, at worst one may also take a cab."[lii]

r. "representation through the minute or the minutest element"
"The doctor who had been summoned to help the baroness in her confinement declared that the critical moment had not yet arrived, and proposed to the baron that they play a game of cards in the adjoining room in the meantime. After awhile, the doleful cry of the baroness reached the ears of the men. 'Ah, mon Dieu, que je souffre!' The husband jumped up, but the physician stopped him saying, 'That's nothing; let us play on.' A little while later, the woman in labor was heard again: 'My God, my God, what pains!' 'Don't you want to go in, Doctor?' asked the baron. 'By no means, it is not yet time,' answered the doctor. At last there rang from the adjacent room the unmistakable cry, 'A-a-a-ai-e-e-e-e-e-E-E-E!' The physician quickly threw down the cards and said, 'Now it's time.'"[liii]

s. "comparison"
e.g., "It is almost impossible to carry the torch of truth through a crowd without singeing somebody's beard."[liv]

t. "representation through absurdity"
e.g., "The motives for our actions may be arranged like the

thirty-two winds, and their names may be classified in a similar way, e.g., Bread-bread-glory or Glory-glory-bread." (Lichtenberg)[lv]

—also questionable as a form of wit

Freud then turns to the "tendencies" of wit. He observes, "Wherever wit is not a means to its end, i.e., harmless, it puts itself in the service of but two tendencies which may themselves be united under one viewpoint; it is either *hostile* wit serving as an aggression, satire, or defense, or it is *obscene* wit serving as a sexual exhibition."[lvi] The aggressive tendency is important because it finds pleasure in what civilization censors. This includes the use of ridicule to expose a hypocritical opponent. That is, the wit-maker finds pleasure in making the bigot look ridiculous. As Freud puts it: "Wit permits us to make our enemy ridiculous through that which we could not utter loudly or consciously on account of existing hindrances; in other words, *wit affords us the means of surmounting restrictions and of opening up otherwise inaccessible sources of pleasure.*"[lvii]

An example is as follows: "Wendell Phillips, according to a recent biography by Lorenzo Sears, was on one occasion lecturing in Ohio, and while on a railroad journey going to keep one of his appointments met in the car a number of clergymen returning from some sort of convention: One of the ministers, feeling called upon to approach Mr. Phillips, asked him, 'Are you Mr. Phillips?' 'I am sir.' 'Are you trying to free the niggers?' 'Yes, sir; I am an abolitionist.' 'Well, why do you preach your doctrines up here? Why don't you go over into Kentucky?' 'Excuse me, are you a preacher?' 'I am, sir.' 'Are you trying to save souls from hell?' 'Yes, sir, that's my business.' 'Well, why don't you go there?'"[lviii]

Harmless wit, in contrast, is innocent and abstract. It qualifies as wit because of its technique and is thus distinguishable from the tendentious variety. Freud offers the following example: "Not only did he not believe in ghosts, but once he was afraid of them."[lix] Such wit hurts no one. It rather elicits pleasure because of its technique of conveying a fear we normally repress. Harmless wit tends to be neutral and is devoid of a cutting edge. This creates a problem for Freud. "If it be true," he says, "that the pleasure created by wit is dependent upon technique on the one hand, and upon tendency on the other, under what common point of view can these two utterly different pleasure-sources of wit be united?"[lx]

In response to his question, Freud distinguishes the pleasure originating in wit-technique from that originating in wit-tendency. He hopes to discover the "mechanism of this resultant pleasure."[lxi] Tendentious wit, he observes, gives pleasure to the extent it overcomes inhibitions that could not otherwise be overcome without a considerable degree of "psychic expenditure." An "economy in the expenditure of inhibitions or suppressions"[lxii] thus occurs with an accompanying sense of pleasure. This is true whether the tendency of wit is "externally" directed (e.g., against institutions or the rich and powerful) or "internally" located (as in the aesthetic alleviation of an "inner feeling" that resists the wish to be directly hostile).

Anticipating a similar explanation of harmless wit (i.e., that derived from the wit-technique), Freud focuses on a variety of types. Among these are witticisms which (1) stress the sound of a word (or words) instead of its meaning; (2) uncover the familiar ("recognition") "where one expects to find something new instead,"[lxiii] and (3) use "modes of reasoning unsanctioned by logic."[lxiv] The third includes intentionally false logic, displacement, absurdity, representation through the opposite, etc. In all three, as in wit-tendency, there is an *economy of psychic expenditure*. They either provide relief from the further spending of energies that are already in the process of being spent or, in anticipation, reduce the extent of effort about to be required. Therein lies the source of pleasure common to all wit that Freud calls "the pleasure mechanism."

The psychogenesis of this mechanism is "play" and/or "jest." It is present in the child's earliest experimentation with words and thoughts. "Playing with words and thoughts, motivated by certain pleasures in economy" (e.g., repetition or similarities and the pleasantness of sound-associations) thus becomes the first stage of wit.[lxv] Significantly, "this playing is stopped by the growing strength of a factor which may well be called criticism or reason. The play is then rejected as senseless or as directly absurd, and by virtue of reason it becomes impossible."[lxvi] Wit thus develops from childhood impulses that: (1) strive to elude reason; and (2) would substitute an infantile state of mind for adulthood. Freud playfully describes wit's actualization of such impulses as the "liberation of nonsense."

The jest, as a second stage in the development of wit, tries "to bring about the resultant pleasure of playing and at the same time appease the protesting reason which strives to suppress the pleasant feeling."[lxvii] The jest shares this trait with wit. The jest is different from wit only to the extent that it is not as aesthetically pleasing (i.e., witty). Also, the jest seeks merely to create pleasure and therefore is not *purposeful in relation* to *thought* (as is wit).

Wit, in contrast, is never without purpose even if its type is harmless and therefore not "tendentious" (Freud's earlier use of the word). That is, at deeper levels of meaning wit's purpose is always to enhance the thought that creates the possibility of play. Wit protects that thought from the inhibiting restrictions of critical judgment or reason. "Where the argument seeks to draw the hearer's reason to its side, wit strives to push aside this reason."[lxviii] Freud calls this the "sense" of wit and considers it to be central to wit's "psychogenesis."

Freud's most intriguing comments are on the excesses of reason. To the extent therapy discerns the meaning of irrational behavior, it tries to bridge the gap between reason and nonsense. "The power of reason," Freud writes, "usually grows so strong during the later part of childhood and during that period of education which extends over the age of puberty, that the pleasure in 'freed nonsense' rarely dares manifest itself. One fears to utter nonsense . . . "[lxix] Freud's dismay is over the oppression of natural instincts by the inhibiting logic of a scientific Geist.

Freud is bold enough in his identification with wit to speculate on the immorality of reason devoid of pleasure. This is surprising considering the rational bent of his thought. Freud laments, "The 'pleasure in nonsense,' as we may call it for short, is, in the seriousness of our life, crowded back almost to the vanishing point."[lxx] Indeed, "Reason, which has stifled the pleasure in nonsense, has become so powerful that not even temporarily can it be abandoned without a toxic agency ... The hilarious humor, whether due to endogenous origin or whether produced toxically, weakens the inhibiting forces, among which is reason, and thus, again makes accessible pleasure-sources, which are burdened by suppression."[lxxi]

What Freud terms the psychogenesis of wit is discernible in its active realization and conceptual intent (*telos*). Wit arises from word play as the liberation of nonsense. Its intent is to guard pleasure from suppression "through reason."[lxxii] That is, "wit carries out its purpose in advancing the thought by magnifying it and guarding it against reason."[lxxiii] Therapy abuses Freud at this point. Therapy's tendency is to strip the client of defenses that deny the power of reason. Such defenses may be essential to emotional well-being. Especially when childlike impulses have been throttled by a punishing parent.

A style of education that diminishes play and daydreaming is an example. Education's regrettable tendency is to foster a hard-headed realism that is blind to creativity. As Freud puts it, the child "makes use of play in order to withdraw from the pressure of critical reason. More powerful, however, are the restrictions which must develop in education along the lines of right thinking, and in the separation of reality from fiction, and it is for this reason that the resistance against the pressures of thinking and reality is far-reaching and persistent."[lxxiv]

Freud notes further traits of wit in his conclusion. He admits that other motives than obtaining pleasure affect wit, and he calls them "subjective." Only a few are genuinely witty, he says, and among these there seem to be present symptoms of neurosis (e.g., dissociated personalities or nervous affections). However, "we certainly cannot maintain that such a psycho-neurotic constitution is a regular or necessary subjective condition for witmaking."[lxxv] The instruction to therapy here is simple. Affirm the witty person in the light of the uniqueness of his/her gift.

Another consideration is that impulse "which strives to complete the mysterious process of wit-formation by imparting it to another."[lxxvi] I like Freud using words like mysterious.* They don't fit the stereotypes that Freud's English translators have forced us to swallow. Curious too is wit's withdrawal from the laughter it produces. What is the role of the other person in this process? Why does the wit-maker not laugh at his own witticism?

The hearer, Freud concludes, laughs to the extent that his unarticulated thoughts are spontaneously released (i.e., laughed away). The witmaker doesn't laugh because to do so would: (1) reduce the amount of pleasure obtained from making the witticism in the first place; and (2) disrupt the "suspension of inhibition cathexis"[lxxvii] at work in the hearer. Thus, "the conditions for laughter are such that a sum of psychic energy hitherto employed in the cathexis of some pathos may experience free discharge."[lxxviii] I am not sure these conditions are present when being witty myself. But they make a great theory.

Other conditions relevant to wit's role in therapy include: a similar set of inhibitions in both the speaker and listener; an intensification of the inhibitions to be released beforehand; an imprecise understanding of the exact nature of the process that's taking place; "the Janus-like double-facedness of wit, which safeguards its original resultant pleasure against the impugnment of critical reason"[lxxix]; a resistance to analysis; a movement toward economy of psychic expenditure; and a sympathetic ear.

Freud concludes that wit, like comedy and humor, seeks a euphoria that can never be recaptured. Eat your heart out, romantics. Wit is an unfulfilled longing for "the state of our childhood in

---

* We forget in America that Freud was primarily a philosopher in a practical profession. He after all was awarded the Goethe Prize of Literature because of his mastery of the German language.

which we did not know the comic, were incapable of wit, and did not need humor to make us happy."[lxxx] Humor is thus the fallen state of childlike contentment. "If we are in a situation which tempts us to liberate painful affects according to our habits," Freud adds, "and motives then urge us to suppress these affects *in statu nascendi*, we have the conditions for humor."[lxxxi]

Freud's words relate directly to therapy. That is, humor can assist the client in easing the burden of quite painful emotions. When the choice is between crying and laughing it may be helpful to laugh. Such laughter releases the pain the client represses in relation to his/her ability to cry. The proximity of crying to laughing (even as tears) implies a connection that enhances the possibility of both.

Freud also grasps the primacy of humor as a subjective process. He writes, "Humor is the most self-sufficient of the comic forms; its process consummates itself in 'one single person' and the participation of another adds nothing new to it. I can enjoy the pleasure of humor originating in myself without feeling the necessity of imparting it to another."[lxxxii] Such characteristics cannot be taken lightly.

We live in a culture that stresses autonomy to the point of isolation. Deprived of authentic community, most of our waking moments are spent alone. Isolation and its accompanying *ennui* is our lonely condition. It is not a moot point that humor engenders a subjectively informed contentment that can conquer isolation. The Zen Buddhists call such contentment *satori*. The term implies an awareness that immediately grasps and celebrates the absurd as the inward realization of joy. I have met therapists who communicate such joy without so much as blinking an eye. They are worthy of emulation because of their mastery of the art of humor as therapy.

Finally, I disagree with Freud's placement of humor's "psychic location in the foreconscious, whereas wit, as we had to assume is formed as a compromise between the unconscious and foreconscious."[lxxxiii] Bracketing Freud's obscure explanation, I question the closer proximity of humor to conscious awareness. Freud's aim was to elevate humor in the light of its reflective nature. But this aim betrays Freud's own repression of feeling to the degree humor is intimately linked to the primary process.

Humor is a more fluid energy than either wit or the comic. It is deeply implanted in the unconscious and is likely the source of both. Its origin is "primitive" in the best sense of the word. (Freud, by the way, used the term as an insult.) What is closer to the surface (e.g., wit and comedy) more readily fits Freud's use of "function" and economy. Humor does not so readily fit. The healing power of humor lies in its subjective depth. Only a few of the existentialists have clearly described this depth. Humor naturally unfolds in a way closer to Schleiermacher's view of feeling as a dimension of awareness.

At bottom there is no such thing as a humorous *thing*. There is rather humor as a quality of subjective perception. Freud's more objective concern is conscious control. He logically elevates ego as function (e.g., in rational relation to an object) without giving the fluidity of humor its intuitive due. Even so, Freud rightly deciphers the dissimilarity of humor from comedy and wit. Humor possesses "a peculiarity which perhaps we have not hitherto emphasized strongly enough."[lxxxiv]

I have spent time exploring *Wit and Its Relation to the Unconscious* because of Freud's seminal influence on therapy and our awareness of life. Why, I wonder, do those who quote Freud have such a feeble grasp of the book's content? It is the most neglected of his books, but in many ways the most profound. No less a critic than Marcuse considers it to be Freud's most creative piece of writing. My hunch is that strict Freudians feel threatened by irrational tendencies that don't fit their ironclad system. They are also very often obsessive-compulsive and could benefit from a little wit and humor.

Freud would roll over in his grave, I think, upon seeing the ossification of his views by the medical establishment. We forget he was a philosopher first and a doctor second, even as death was the wish he directly confronted. Freud was a humanist and skeptical of medical methods, as seen in every essay in *Character and Culture*. English translations of his work have been sadly remiss in this regard. How can we explain such richly pliant symbols as *mutterlieb* (mother-womb) reaching our mother-tongue in as literal a form as "uterus"? We forget that Freud's claim to fame in the German-speaking world was the Goethe prize of *literature*. So it goes.

The version of Freud that filters down to therapy is cold, critical, serious and absurdly cautious. Freudian fundamentalists cling to the force (dogma) of his language without regard for his more spirited intent (meaning). As Bettelheim notes:

> It became apparent to me that the English renditions of Freud's writings distort much of the essential humanism that permeates the originals . . . Freud often spoke of the soul—of its nature and structure, its development, its attributes, how it reveals itself in all we do and dream . . . Nearly all his many references to the soul, and to matters pertaining to soul, have been excised in translation . . . Psychoanalysis becomes in English translations something that refers and applies to others as a system of intellectual constructs. Therefore, students of psychoanalysis are not led to take it personally—they are not moved to gain access to their own unconscious and everything else within them that is most human but is nevertheless unacceptable to them . . . Freud wanted to make clear that psychoanalysis was concerned not just with man's body and his intellect, as his medical colleagues were, but—and most of all—which forms such a large part of the soul of living man—or, to put it in classical terms, with that unknown netherworld in which, according to ancient myths, the souls of men dwell.[lxxxv]

To grasp Freud's love of wit requires embracing the humanitarian impulse of his thought. This impulse includes the likes of spontaneity, play, nonsense and humor. Implications for therapy are obvious. W. S. Maugham cuts to the quick of Freud's intent when he blurts: "Impropriety is the soul of wit." The question that remains: Did Freud snicker?

Humor's role is to soothe the pain of confrontation with personal affirmation. It follows that healthy laughter, as one expression of humor, can be wholly in accord with humor. Yet laughter can also be the clanging cymbal of humor's opposite. When blind to kindness, and sarcastic, hostile or cruel, such laughter can cut like a stiletto. A decent therapist knows the paradoxical difference. When in tune with genuine concern, humor can be a powerful agent of healing. I think of the request of the Spanish writer, Camilo José Cela, upon receiving the Nobel Prize. He wanted his epitaph to read: "Here lies someone who tried to screw his fellow man as little as possible."

CHAPTER X

I COULD HAVE DIED LAUGHING

> "Our cares are the mothers, not only of our charities and virtues, but of our best joys and most cheering and enduring pleasures"
>
> —W. G. Simms

A unique feature of humor is its access to an alternative field of perception. The maze of activities we so seriously pursue conceals a tragic vision that humor intuits beyond. When neurosis breeds anxious movement, humor relaxes. Humor triggers insights we might not otherwise consider. It discerns the presence of mind to enjoy the moment. Humor pierces the neurosis our compulsivity hides. It enhances personal courage in the face of despair. What enables humor to work its spell?

AMBIGUITY

One answer is humor's tolerance of ambiguity. Ambiguity arises from the confusing nature of emotional events that make us human. These events include the unconscious effect of external limits that lie beyond rational control. The most obvious, and therefore concealed, source of ambiguity is death.

Death threatens our facade of self-sufficiency. It reminds us that our lives are fleeting, temporal, and finite. It challenges the worth of our treasured autonomy. What's the point of being free if all we do is die? Death renders absurd our manipulation of external events in order to repress what is *ultimately ambiguous*. For this reason we hide from death's conscious sting. We pretend that death happens to other people. Or we "bury" ourselves in work to avoid the ambiguity that death raises. But a sign of maturity is our tolerance of ambiguous feeling. Humor curiously increases such tolerance. Even death is less of an ogre when viewed with humorous eyes.

To encourage humor, however, creates a problem. Humor confronts the patient's expectation that "If I'm miserable, you'd better be miserable too." Patients often take humor as the insult of not being taken seriously. In fact the opposite is true. To respond with humor is to take the patient seriously enough to respect him as a person with a sense of humor. Humor gets beneath the rigidity that denies the pleasure of humor in the first place. The person who is obsessively concrete is an obvious example. But even "literalists" can be coaxed to enjoy the ambiguity of humor. That is, humor can be taught and understood as a gift. Its realization can free repression and even tame the ambiguity of death.

Maslow notes that without an awareness of death we would be unable to love. For death gives clarity to love in the context of the brevity of life.* The same is true of humor, and at an elementary level. The simpleminded, for example, can grasp the relation of humor to basic emotions that include our fear of death. They are often more perceptive than the egghead who catches every detail but misses THE BIG PICTURE. As Kierkegaard puts it, to exist in the truth means "to make sure of what the simplest of men also knows."[lxxxvi] Evolving therapy to an honest exchange of humor is thus a major step toward mastering ambiguity.

As a role model the therapist has every right to enjoy himself. Otherwise he/she is teaching neurosis. A belly laugh can be instructive and puts ambiguity in perspective. It also helps the therapist maintain his balance. It conveys the message: "Hey, I know

---

* Cf. Jean Wright's intriguing work on the relevance of humor to pastoral counseling in the context of mortality and themes derived from the Bible. Also, Hyers' study from the angle of Christian theology on Zen and the Comic Spirit.

it's crazy out there. It's crazy for me too. But a good way of handling the craziness is with a sense of humor. And for God's sake, stop taking yourself and the situations you can't control, so seriously."

DREAMS

A second point is humor's proximity to the world of dreams. Dreams can be an invaluable source of self-discovery. What the client describes as "only a dream" is often a clear glimpse of unconscious needs and creative channels of growth. Too strict an adherence to "the reality principle" aborts such growth. Scornful of what can't be proved (i.e., *fiction*), the reality principle pits itself against the imagination. It reflects the modern tendency to dismiss "myth" as the opposite of truth. To look askance at myth betrays an outdated "naturalism." In the light of Freud and Jung, "empirical facts" arising from rational investigation are clearly of no greater value than the mythico-religious themes that dreamlife reveals.

That the dream world is not outwardly "seen" does not diminish its importance. The dream can blend and weave irrational threads of experience that objective analysis *overlooks*. It taps a vein of imaginative clarity that is as profound and as old as antiquity. The dream gives meaning to themes in the human story that each self is living.

Such themes are too numerous to mention. They begin with the earliest premonitions of childhood and are likely archetypal. They may appear in the kindly form of a father figure who gives solace in time of need. Or they may abruptly startle *à la* the recurring nightmare of an earthquake, or being chased by a tornado. Whatever their form, they are an ingredient of emotional reality worth exploring. They offer a clear glimpse of the unconscious that might otherwise stay hidden. They are also "fun." A frequent result of their denial is depression.

While dreams should be taken seriously, they should also be taken with a humorous grain of salt. The client who is overly intense in his portrayal of a "bad" dream, for example, needs help in de-mystifying its scary side. Simply relating the dream is a first step, especially in the case of a nightmare. The therapist can verify the anxiety a nightmare raises, and be the outlet of its expression. A nightmare's emotional impact is diffused via the simple act of putting it into words. The more shocking the image thrust to conscious awareness, the greater is the need to verbalize its content. A disturbing image is a subliminal condensation of unconscious fears. A dream is a symbolic transformation of experience into meaning, as a nightmare is an intuitive reconstruction of the demonic.

The habitat of dreams in turn is no more serious than everyday existence. Even a horrifying dream contains redeemable themes that can be humorously freed. Freud's insight that dreams can play a joke on the conscious mind, in a way similar to wit and its relation to the unconscious, is suggestive. I have found many a nocturnal monster to be a trickster in wolf's clothing. The tradition of the trickster is filled with examples of such and can be a lively theme for therapy.

My therapeutic arsenal includes a grasp of legends and myths that penetrate the mask of fright with prankish humor (as in Radin's *The Trickster*). Such myths are one of many ways to delve beneath demonic projections. Nightmares have a healing purpose. The key is to look the demon squarely in the eye and ask him if he can spare a chuckle. Dreaming represents a pre-reflective alternative to common sense reality. It in no sense is entirely serious. Humor is a medium of access to the symbolic world that dreams reveal.

HOPE

Humor is a context for tempering the obsession of psychology with morbidity and sickness. The problematic view of man as *homo pathologicus* became conscious in thought for good reason. Namely, the nineteenth century's overemphasis of the good, the true, and the beautiful. This overemphasis embellished the lighter side of man, in the name of rationality and progress, without respecting his darker, more ambiguous nature.

Freudian thought is a natural corrective in this regard. It functions as a systematic application of what Nietzsche terms "idealizing in the direction of ugliness." Amidst the ensuing collapse of western values, Freud obsesses on the deviant dangers of libidinal urges without a reasoning ego. Europe is the patient, and psychoanalysis is the immunity Freud invents to effect a cure.

The likelihood of war and the subsequent victimization of the Jew is more than a historical footnote. Freud is fearful of both. He sees repression as a symptom of social disintegration. He makes pathology conscious in order to heighten the awareness in Western man of his potential for brutality and self-destruction. (Augustine makes a like use of "original sin" at an earlier juncture in history.) The failure of Freud's medicine to work its cure surfaces with a vengeance *à la* Adolf Hitler. Needless to say, it becomes difficult for man heartily to laugh.

Freud sensed this difficulty in his designation of humor as the *summum bonum* of risible pleasure. The distinction he makes between wit, comedy and humor is often neglected. So is the context of his later essay on humor (1928). Freud is facing cancer of the jaw. Like the condemned prisoner he writes about, he shows no sign of depression or resentment. Freud transcends his fate with the jest of writing an essay on humor. Humor and its affirmation is a paradigm of the direction in which the dying Freud would point Western culture. The depressed state of the German economy parallels his remedy for "depression." Freud reminds us of humor's role as an escape valve ("gallows" humor) amidst social upheaval.

A redemptive motif is also present. It appears to the extent Freud gives himself "up" out of concern for the whole. His intent parallels "crucifixion" and "resurrection" in Christian theology. As Kierkegaard puts it: "A man who lets himself be skinned alive in order to show how the humorous smile is produced by the contraction of a particular muscle—and thereupon follows this with a lecture on humor."[1] Like Freud, Kierkegaard intuits the necessary relation of humor to the dimension of depth in mental illness. His cure includes an acceptance of pain and death for a higher calling. Both thinkers move beyond a preoccupation with self to a sacrificial altruism that lets them become the self for others.

The concern of humor is at once more emotional than rational. It reveals, gives space to, and reflectively affirms feeling. It does so simply, deeply, and paradoxically. It thus speaks directly *and indirectly* the language of the heart and soul. The laughter humor elicits resists the impact of an impersonal world. As Conrad Hyers puts it:

> . . . Our sense of the awful nearness of catastrophe lies close to the heart of the imagination today. But it does not paralyze the heart itself. At the very heart of man there lies a humane perspective rooted not quite in hope but in a hope about hope! . . . Laughter is hope's last weapon. Crowded on all sides with idiocy and ugliness . . . we seem nonetheless to nourish laughter as our only remaining defense. In the presence of disaster and death we laugh instead of crossing ourselves. Or perhaps better stated, laughter is our way of crossing ourselves.[lxxxvii]

Therapy can enhance the power of such laughter and enable the client to come to terms with tragedy. Viewing tragedy in a way that remains open to humor, the therapist can facilitate the transition from an ironic position to one of hope. Instead of denying tragedy, humor embraces its meaning fully and attempts to move beyond it.

"Humor," says Kierkegaard: "has its justification in its tragic side, in the fact that it reconciles itself to the pain, which despair seeks to abstract from, although it knows no way out."[lxxxviii] He has hit the nail on the head. In the context of tragedy, the therapist can be a bridge of feeling between irony and humor; the patient can test the existence of this bridge, and at his/her own pace embrace or reject its meaning.

A therapist with a sense of humor is also more able to engender a sense of self-worth and meaning. When empathic enough to cultivate humor in others, he can be a source of acceptance that was missing in childhood. Instead of reviving inner voices of doubt, the therapist can encourage a "transference" that heals doubt's impact in the comforting light of humor. This parallels Freud's notion that through humor the super-ego "speaks . . . kindly words of comfort to the intimidated ego."[lxxxix]

Freud's words approach the Christian notion of grace and remind us of humor's ability to conquer guilt. The grace humor conveys is self-acceptance regardless of merit or moral weakness. Humor puts guilt in such a perspective that its relativity jumps out at us. We are reminded through humor of the essential absurdity of guilt in its fixation on this or that shortcoming. Via a humor that in Kierkegaard's phrase "comprehends guilt-consciousness as a totality," we are momentarily freed of the feeling that we don't measure up. We are able to recognize guilt as a self-imposed affliction. Demeaning obsessions on a particular act can be seen in the light of a deeper self that — transcends our need to be punished. Humor awakens the awareness that, despite our frailties, "we are accepted" (Tillich).

Our frailties are what make us human. They are as laughable as they are a cause of remorse. They remind us that at times it's as easy to laugh as it is to cry. On occasion, in fact, we do both at once, as humor reconciles us to our follies. Humor touches a subliminal chord of feeling that forgets instead of regrets. Amidst the guilt of falling short of good intentions (in-tensions), humor views all guilt as but one theme in a larger cosmic drama. It discerns an ultimate resolution that transcends the conclusion we are insignificant or worthless.

Humor offers an alternative to the logic of despair. It frees felt inadequacies that more rigid approaches reinforce. That is, humor moves beyond medicine's hardheaded fixation on morbidity and disease. Instead of insisting on a pathology to fit a behavioral symptom, humor values the uniqueness of each individual. Genuine humor raises hope in what Frankl calls "man's search for meaning." It discerns that in all of life's absurdity there exists a caring source of acceptance. Hyers phrases this nicely. "Without faith," he says:

> "... humor becomes superficial, empty and helpless. Laughter turns into mockery, banter into blasphemy, comedy and tragedy. Humor passes over into despair if it has no groundedness in the sacred, if it is not essentially and inwardly related to holy things. But if it has this foundation, it can play its own peculiar role in the inner dialectic of the sacred and the comic."[xc]

LOVE AND LAUGHTER

The meaning of faith here, in the more rational focus of therapy, must remain an open question. That humor is "inner" in a sense similar to the sacred, however, is poignant. Hyers' "inner dialectic of the sacred and the comic" points to the proximity of humor to our deepest emotions. These emotions are therapeutic agents whose symbolic richness humor unearths. Humor personally paints the world, as it were, in the colors of meaning, hope, and self-acceptance.

What links us most directly to our fellow creatures is the inwardness of feeling. "I have always maintained," says Kierkegaard, "that all men have equal access to passion and feeling."[xci] (1848) Hence, "The religious speaker" (for our purposes therapist) "should be distinguished by his having existentially made sure of what the simplest of men also knows."[xcii] The instruction here to therapy is that humor is a "simple" process. Humor begs the Socratic question and evokes obvious feeling that has been obscured. To the extent humor opens the inwardness of feeling, the concerned therapist is sensitive to its presence.

A progenitor of Freud, Friedrich Nietzsche, casts humor in a similar light. During his struggle to remain sane and not give in to suicidal tendencies, he makes a telling discovery. He discovers in himself the need to learn to laugh. He lashes out at the absurd seriousness of an age that demeans the value of laughter. He says through the mouth of Zarathustra:

> "You higher men, the worst about you is that you have not learned to dance as one must dance —- dancing away over yourselves! What does it matter that you are failures? How much is still possible! So learn to laugh away over yourselves! Lift up your hearts, you good dancers, high, higher! And do not forget good laughter. This crown of him who laughs, this rose-wreath crown: to you, my brothers, I throw this crown. Laughter I have pronounced holy; you higher men, learn to laugh."[xciii]

Zarathustra's directive cuts in several directions. It reminds us of the importance of not taking life and our assigned roles in life too seriously. In the context of Nietzsche's own struggle with madness, his words convey a desperate longing. Namely, to overcome the apparent meaninglessness of human existence. Whether he succeeds in this task is doubtful. More important to us is his discovery of laughter. He sees laughter as a means of relieving the *burden* of despair.

To abort the chance of sharing a good laugh is a mistake. With ready-made rationalizations, it cuts short the healing power of humor. Such therapy adheres too strictly to the rule of minimizing external stimulation. It ignores humor as an avenue of healing and confuses humor with insensitivity. Yet healthy humor, because of its simple grounding in feeling, is very sensitive and can be very soft-spoken. Humor also coaxes engagement with the real world. Humor can plant a seed of hope, even when the client does not immediately respond.

I'm not saying that humor must be overtly present in therapy. There are times when the possession of a sense of humor *requires silence*. To be authentic, humor must seriously confront destructive behavior. Such behavior often masquerades as humor, but is at root a negation of humor's intent; because it mocks vulnerability. Vulnerability must be protected in order to preserve the possibility of humor. Nor is humor a magic panacea that cures all neurosis in a single bound. It is rather a perspective, a way of tilting our feelers toward the human sounds around us. And through humor the person can begin to feel better about being human.

Humor's grasp of the human condition is creative and translatable. It can be implanted, nourished, and take root from within. It is grounded in an emotional stability that is reflective and thoughtfully values the sacredness of life. Humor puts the impact of tragedy in a more manageable light.

The arrow Nietzsche flings at academicians could as easily find a target in the therapist. To the extent that care is a necessary ingredient of therapy, care's absence buttresses a stance that harms the playful instincts. As Nietzsche more emphatically puts it:

> "What has so far been the greatest sin here on earth? Was it not the word of him who said, 'Woe unto those who laugh here'? Did he himself find no reason on earth for laughing? Then he searched very badly. Even a child could find reasons here. He did not love enough: else he would also have loved us who laugh. But he hated and mocked us: howling and gnashing of teeth he promised."[xciv]

Nietzsche's allusion to a child is suggestive. He reminds us of the requirement that therapy be simple without being simplistic. Therapy should be in touch with childlike emotions that are entirely simple in their origin. This does not mean childish regression or a selfish disregard of others. It means a reintegration of the self with the reverie of childhood, and an honest acceptance of what is most human. In the words of William Penn: "They that love beyond the world cannot be separated by it." The ultimate concern humor discerns is being kind from within.

CHAPTER XI

CHUCKLED ABSTRACTIONS

> "Humor signifies the triumph not only of the ego but also of the pleasure principle."
> — Sigmund Freud

I suggest you peruse this chapter as you would a menu, and pick and choose. When I have a thought about humor, I write it down. What follows is a collection of such thoughts, arranged at random in diary form. Some are clinical, some spout theory, and some are just wacky ideas. My list of WHAT HUMOR IS and WHAT HUMOR IS NOT (a nice idea for groups) may be of special interest.

HALLUCINATIONS

Humor is helpful in demystifying the frightening side of sense hallucinations. A therapy open to humor views the patient as a total person of which the hallucination is one expression. Humor thus offers an alternative to viewing hallucinations with a jaundiced eye. More common than people think, hallucinations can be a source of shame, and trigger the fear in the patient that he/she is abnormal and "insane." An effective approach is to view hallucinations as a natural break in the continuum of day-to-day existence.

A HUMORLESS EXCEPTION

An exception to my success with humor is the heroin addict. My observation is based on briefly working at a methadone treatment center. I have never dealt with a tougher population, and I don't envy those who do it on a full time basis. A reason may be my fondness of humor. The heroin addict is so enmeshed in a world of manipulation that he/she is unable to appreciate the humor of others. His alienation is *absolute* and he is unable to enjoy the pleasures of normal experience. His laughter is often sadistic, and a far cry from healthy humor. John Belushi is an exception and a tragic example.

COMEDY, WIT AND HUMOR

Humor is the best medicine for gravity and is akin to (a kin to) comedy. Comedy tickles us on a visual plane, for example, in a play. We respond facially by smiling at what strikes us on the surface as amusing. Philosophically, humor is both higher and lower than "the comical" in relation to the depth it ponders. The levity humor more thoroughly enjoys is heightened by the absurd at the level of feeling, where comedy loses its footing in the absurd. Comedy can heighten our grasp of humor's resolution of the absurd. It also, ironically, touches gravity as in "the tragi-comic." Both, practically, tickle funnybones that lift depression. Wit is similar, but more conceptual; it is competitively focused on oral needs as a kind of verbal fencing. It can retrieve reverie from the mouth of humor in the likeness of a gull pecking a fish. Wit is rapidly conscious and generally harmless. Wit can also be vicious and sharply sting. Both forms of wit typify what it means to be "quick-witted." Harmless wit has been nurtured on love and is a first cousin of humor as distinguished above. Most wit is unwittingly grounded in health (in the likeness of a Mark Twain) and is what we mean when we say a person has a "good wit."

HOW OBJECTIVE ARE WE?

Therapy is a close range encounter that can never reach fruition in the ether of "objective" abstraction. Objectivity in a technical sense, because all knowledge by definition is "personal," *in reality does not exist*. What we call "objectivity" in common sense language is of course important. It is how we view the forest to discern a path of individuation amidst the trees. But objectivity is only an approximation of what our personal feelings "objectify" as a thought. Its practical function is to "bracket" emotions that are "too hot to handle."

Hostile jabs at the core of my being, for example, are tough to absorb. Especially when they hit close to home and might be true. Hostility requires a mechanics of diffusion that numbs the sting of its immediate impact. Being *objective* gives space to a reflective detachment that can then orient a more open encounter.

An objective stance is also helpful in structuring manipulative types who play fast and loose with the truth. Such persons remind me of greased ball bearings. They are so *slick* and adept at evasion that all you're left with is a maze of double-talk not worth hearing. The opposite danger of objectivity is assuming the rigidity of its method. Analyzing "things" from a humorless distance is a manipulation in kind that shrinks the possibility of humor. In therapeutic lingo, objectivity mistakes neurosis and schizophrenia for sociopathy. Too strict an adherence to objectivity betrays a serious deficiency in Soul.

YOU HAVE A HOLE IN YOUR SOUL

I would never trust a therapist who seemed lacking in Soul. Working through protected vulnerabilities is too painful a process. Why discard defenses only to discover a therapist who is more defended? Soul implies vulnerability and a sensitive response *to* vulnerability. Everyone of course has Soul. But we moderns have drastically shrunk the conscious skull of its influence. Notice the absence of Soul in "shrinks" whose *modus operandi* is solely reductionistic. Their hard-headed empiricism is a reason *in extremis* that applies to things, and there's the rub. They may be what the doctor ordered for those who suffer from soul *possession* and want to be treated as things.

I AM NOT A THING

An irony of humor as therapy is the chronic victim who has been treated as a "thing" since he was born. His/her self-image is so diminished that he finds security in being badly treated. Such persons prefer the security of rejection to the insecurity of growth. Like the prisoners in Plato's cave, they blindly slay whoever points them to the light outside. Their condition, of course, is pathological. Its cause is childhood tapes so deeply ingrained it requires years of therapy to overcome.

WHAT HUMOR IS NOT

Humor is not hostility.
Humor is not sarcasm.
Humor is not aggressive.
Humor is not racist, sexist, or classist.
Humor is not irony.
Humor is not comedy or wit.
Humor is not arrogance.
Humor is not sociopathic.
Humor is not calculating.
Humor is not a joke.
Humor is not laughter.
Humor is not frenetic.
Humor is not childish.
Humor is not ridicule.
Humor is not selfish.
Humor is not violent.

Humor is not insensitive.
Humor is not inane.
Humor is not manipulative.
Humor is not afraid of death.
Humor is not narcissistic.
Humor is not profane.
Humor is not faith.
Humor is not anger.
Humor is not irrational.
Humor is not mean.
Humor is not insane.
Humor is not banality.
Humor is not anality.
Humor is not folly.
Humor is not unfair.
Humor is not absurd.
Humor is not afraid to cry.
Humor is not stupidity.
Humor is not tragic.
Humor is not a cow, a pig, or a duck.

Humor is not any of the above but it can be present in varying degrees in irony, comedy, wit, a joke, laughter, inanity, profanity, faith, anger, foolishness, insanity, banality, anality, folly, absurdity, stupidity, tragedy, a phallus, a cow, a pig, or a duck.

HUMOR IS

Humor is playful.
Humor is hopeful.
Humor is open.
Humor is funny.
Humor is kind.
Humor is gentle.
Humor is no respecter of rank or privilege.

Humor is empathic.
Humor is childlike.
Humor is healthy.
Humor is gullibly smart.
Humor is ridiculous.
Humor is empathic.
Humor is forgiving.
Humor is non-sense.
Humor is sensitive.
Humor is in dialogue with the sacred.
Humor is non-rational.
Humor is ultimately fair.
Humor is faithful.
Humor is free.
Humor is accepting.
Humor is self-accepting.
Humor is frivolous.
Humor is forgiving.
Humor is able to be quiet.
Humor is able to speak aloud.
Humor is ethical.
Humor is comfortable with death.
Humor is self-accepting.
Humor is healing.
Humor is mischievous.
Humor is loving.
Humor is a celebration of life.

I, FOR SOME REASON, LIKE YOU

Liking a patient is important. When a patient rankles me to the point I see no redeeming qualities, I refer him to someone else. What is surprising, however, is that most of my patients manage to embody Will Rogers' claim that "I never met a man I didn't like." No matter how clingy or crude, every person possesses a flicker of dignity worth affirming. When as hard to find as a needle in a haystack, such dignity should still be kept in mind.

Sensitivity to hidden strengths is essential to the patience that the evolution of growth requires. Be it as humble an effort as noting the progress of sweat on the brow of a tedious bore. The labor of humor as therapy is akin to giving birth. It requires patience, imagination, and a visceral strength of will.

B. O. PLENTY

There is of course a time to confront behavior that turns others off in the likeness of B. O. Plenty. Humor is here helpful because it softens the sting of the patient's realization of how obnoxious his behavior actually is. Its secret is a good-natured grasp of the obvious and too quick a movement to humor can trigger defenses. When feeling energetic and in tune with a patient's need, I take the risk. The risk is being spontaneous enough to *outwit* evasion. Wit thus functions as a foil for humor. It is adept at checking slick manipulation. It confronts (con-fronts) the exploitation of feeling that humor's vulnerability allows. A surer way to avoid manipulation is serious reality testing over an extended period of time. Humor is a felt bond whose natural evolution in the course of a relationship is trust. But humor can also shorten the time it takes for trust to reach fruition.

Comedians accomplish this in a social context. They disarm us in a way that elicits personal rapport, and what we recognize in the humor of the comedian is ourselves. We find ourselves laughing at self-disclosures that in exaggerated form are our own. The comedian acts out neurotic anxiety that normal sobriety hides. Thus we are given license to laugh away insecurities we take seriously enough to repress. We have the further right as spectators not to laugh. Our reluctance to laugh may be as simple as *bad* humor and is as much ethical as aesthetic. Don Rickles, for example, strikes me as being hostile, cruel, and not very funny.

Withholding laughter may as clearly reflect a serious malaise.

It can mask brooding resentments in need of ventilation. When this is the case humor and therapy are the same. Even as a humorless therapist may receive more from a humorous client than he/she is able to give in return. Humor as therapy implies the frivolous softening of overly rigid defenses.

The stubbornness of such defenses is unconscious. It has taken years to develop and is cold and numb toward what has been coldly numbed in itself. Namely, the spontaneous enjoyment of pleasure it has been taught to feel as a threat. Withholding laughter in this way is manipulative! It's as subtle as pious bigots who use religion as a hostility stick. Such persons are *absolutely* serious and demand to be taken with *absolute* seriousness. Their god is Death and they cast a righteous eye toward anyone who approaches in the spirit of play. They forget that "faith without laughter leads to dogmatism," and that "laughter without faith leads to cynicism and despair."[xcv]

There is an intellectual version of the same disease. Its victims are disturbed by emotion — to the point of having none (i.e., emotion). Their malady is just as serious and similarly dogmatic. They replace faith with high-sounding rationalization and are hard nuts to crack. That in fact is the problem. They are so absorbed in cracking nuts that all we are left to digest is an empty shell. Intellectuals often read vulnerability as weakness and feel strongest when raising insecurity in others. Their apparent strength is brittle. This becomes clear upon closer inspection of the felt ridicule these lonely people nurture. They defend themselves from pain via self-imposed isolation. Their intellectualizing is childish, and ironically rooted in childhood.

DICE CLAY WHO?

An important contrast is between manipulatively rooted illnesses and those that exist in the victims of manipulation. The first seem rationally based and are without a face-saving (i.e., social) mask. That is, sociopathy expresses the rationality of the whole in aggressive acts of manipulation that society can no longer bear to recognize as an image of itself. Society then classifies them in some sense as criminal or insane. Manipulation *per se* is not what is condemned by the sociopathic label. The label rather factors out manipulation that deviates too strongly from the norm. Sadly, most of us are sociopathic in a "normal" way, to the extent the collective identity of society sanctions our pursuit of self-interest. Because of humor's dependence on an honest exchange of feeling, it is ineffective in treating the sociopath. The sociopath misreads the play of humor as an invitation to exert control over others. Thus humor cannot evolve beyond its aggressive forms as irony and sarcasm.

What is labeled "schizophrenia" is more receptive to humor as an agent of healing. The term of course is ambiguous and has been as over-used in diagnosis as our present fixation on "borderline personality disorder." Even so, schizophrenia can be differentiated from sociopathy as behavior that is interpretive. My fear here is of being misinterpreted myself. I'm speaking of schizophrenia in a social context and am offering a composite of its idealized traits. The danger of such an approach is romanticizing a pathological condition. That is not my intention. I am rather making an archetype of the best traits of schizophrenics I have worked with. That is, I am reading schizophrenia (and schizophrenic projections) *en toto* as if it were a person. And the *worst* traits of schizophrenics I have worked with, not even Van Gogh could sketch.

Schizophrenia's tendency is toward active vulnerability to the world as meaningless and irrational. The schizophrenic is susceptible to a collective fear that is ontologically given. This fear is an unconscious (and repressed) projection of the whole that the schizophrenic has personified as a projection of himself. Because the schizophrenic is vulnerable to this fear, he/she feels compelled to test its truth. The schizophrenic finds himself in a sacrificial position beyond his control. His situation seems as crazy to him as he seems crazy to those who closely inspect him. His inadequacy arises in the absurdity of being *too human.* The schizophrenic is painfully aware of the manipulation of feeling that is the sociopathic norm. He/she has failed to construct a defensive "ego" sufficiently detached from the impact of manipulation.

Such manipulation is the tendency of the age. It considers itself rational and is a guise the schizophrenic can't assume. Reason is power to the same degree the schizophrenic is disempowered by the *unreason* he/she feels. The result is double binds and contradictory impulses that seem beyond resolution. As his anxiety increases he/she may even detach himself from everything external. This is due to an inability to rationally convey the degree of absurdity he/she feels. Such a person is ripe for humor because humor can make sense of *the irrational* at the level of feeling. Humor refutes the over extension of reason via what Freud calls "an economy of expenditure in feeling." The tendency of clinicians to treat schizophrenic symptoms with Skinnerian techniques is at this point a mistake. We fail to distinguish between schizophrenia (ego diffusion) and sociopathy as manipulation (ego infusion). Sociopathy is *a cause* of schizophrenia whose emotional knots humor can loosen.

THOUGHTS OUT OF SEASON

a.

Like jazz, humor occurs in spontaneous relation to improvisation; its musician must be at one with the free flow of energies that give rise to the object of humor's creation. Therapy airs the notes of humor, as it were, only as the spirit moves *in* and *through* the process. The art lies in discerning, and being open to, humor's presence while respecting the hiddenness of its source.

b.

As locked as we are in reductionism, conceptual clarity may be a necessary framework for a freer response to humor. This is one reason I have pursued the role of humor in emotional healing. A problem in all of us perhaps is our inability to appreciate humor when it is presented to us by others.

c.

Does it beg the question to say laughter is nothing to laugh at? Can you tell me why we are at the paradoxical point of triggering a laugh when we do? Or are we by then at the point of pointing out the point that the point is there is no point? Pardon my wit.

d.

As serious as the misuse of humor, is the tendency of many professionals to place humor a little higher than leprosy. They view humor as a "defense mechanism" that hinders communication and "blocks" the exploration of deeper problems. In truth the opposite is true. Humor more often frees communication. To embellish, it can move blocks as big as mountains. As can the open response of a therapist to the humorous aside of a patient. I recall countless examples of a chuckle on my part triggering immediate relaxation.

e.

I disagree with those who in the name of objectivity disregard humor. I'm as good as anyone at exploring serious themes in a quietly critical way. Humor doesn't thwart this process. It rather enhances and is central to it.

f.

To ignore humor is to do the patient a disservice. The questionable aim of such therapy is to get at "real" problems that the therapist feels conceptually equipped to handle. Destructive forms of humor *do* prevent the therapist from performing what he has been trained to see as his professional task. His unthinking tendency, however, is to dismiss *all* humor as evasion, pathology, or both. This, it seems to me, is the most reactionary approach imaginable. It says more about the biases of the therapist than the pathology of the client.

g.

The reduction of humor's multi-faceted identity to a neatly contrived explanation is telling. It points to the inadequacy of models that "inform" the therapist's perception. He/she seems the victim of a self-perpetuating cycle of *academia rigor mortis*. Most of us have spent countless hours pondering sober studies of sober problems under the tutelage of sober experts. No wonder our response to humor is so soberly sophomoric. Our microscopic eyes can't distinguish the humorous forest from the pathological trees.

h.

Our methods of credential gathering encourage an anhedonic condition. We suffer from a blind compulsion to create mountains of research that no one cares a flea's ear about. Our models of thought have grown rational to the point of being complexly absurd. Their tendency is to negate the irrational sides of existence with which humor is naturally in tune. They influence like conclusions at the level of therapy. They ignore the power in humor, recognized since antiquity, to bring health to the soul.

i.

The overly serious assumptions of many theorists reflect the alienation of our times. We seem trapped in a singular sanity requiring the either/or categorization of sickness and health. We have developed a therapy that is obsessive in its adherence to the rational requirements of technological civilization. Such therapy is *one dimensional* and *emotionally unequipped* to cope with the pathological contents it unfortunately exploits. It betrays the modern mania to force nature to be "logical." When it is in reality the chaotic divination of a mischievous musician.

j.

Why do so many physicians deny the illogical origin of paradox? Why are they so inclined to ignore the realm of quarks and disappearing electrons in the Einsteinian world that double messages *are*. All messages after all are multiple. The strength of paradoxical intent is that it recognizes such multiplicity and affirms it.

k.

The therapeutic challenge is to evolve conceptual models of growth that are secure enough in their grounding in reason not to be consumed by the irrational (e.g., in the self-destructive mode of a Nietzsche). Our models must likewise be empathetic enough in their identification with the patient that his/her irrationality can be emotionally embraced.

l.

The self-destructive urges that inform the schizophrenic vision must be affirmed before they can be integrated. I mean this to the extent that their meaning *is* irrational (i.e., as an intuition of the irrationalities of a rational *Weltanschauung*). This can be done without succumbing to their ironic, hopeless, and ultimately paranoid conclusions. Humor, curiously, meets this challenge. It is one of but a few vital energies that are flexible enough in their grasp of the irrational to walk such a tightrope (i.e., of impossible expectations).

m.

That some therapists do not instinctively possess a sense of humor underscores its rarity; and accentuates the importance of giving empathic license to those who do. An effort should be made to open all channels of communication that encourage rather than *dis*courage humor's utilization.

As Freud reminds us:

> "It is not everyone who is capable of the humorous attitude: it is a rare and precious gift, and there are many people who have not even the capacity for deriving pleasure from humor when it is presented to them by others . . . We have still very much to learn about the nature of that energy."[xcvi]

The instruction to therapy here is two-fold. First, there is a perspective in humor that enhances our acceptance of pleasure. Its vision embodies a source of enjoyment that can be shared with another. Second, humor is an energizing agent about which we know very little and of which we should become increasingly conscious. Paradox is an important avenue of humor's actualization.

n.

The client's use of humor as avoidance (e.g., as an "escape mechanism") can be helpful. There's nothing wrong with avoiding what is potentially dangerous. If humor fends off callused intrusion to facilitate healing, it's appropriate. My distinction is between *being defensive* and *feeling defenseless*. The former is obstinate and abuses humor. The latter amounts to helplessness and needs humor to buttress what are fragile and necessary defenses.

o.

All of us, after all, are too amply defended. Whatever gives us security — be it home, status, ideas, etc., — is a defense against insecurity. The final insecurity we defend ourselves against, and against which there's no defense but life itself, is death.* Thus a humorous response to the needless stripping of defenses (without which we feel "defenseless") is justified.

p.

Laughing at oneself carries the danger of masochism. It is important that the client's attempts at humor not degenerate (especially in groups) to the level of self-abuse.

---

* I recently attended a conference on "Humor and Pastoral Care" jointly sponsored by the American Association for Therapeutic Humor and the Institute for the Advancement of Human Behavior. I bounced from seminar to seminar in serendipitous fashion on topics as wide-ranging as: "Humor in Homiletics", "Humor and Near Death Experiences", and "Jewish Humor" (via the adroit insights of Rabbi Joseph Telushkin), "Humor in Public Worship," "Reconciliation and Humor,"etc. I came to realize that each speaker had directly confronted the personal question of death by way of his/her own "sense" of humor.

q.
There are cases on record of "hypomania" as a response to humor. Because of the tendency in humor to raise unresolved trauma, the hypomaniac is unable to tolerate its presence. When experiencing its emotion, he may lose control of his/her muscles and even faint. I have heard of such occurrences but they are rare. They would require obvious caution and suggest a natural limit to humor's effectiveness.

r.
There is an undeniable power in laughter that directly taps primary emotions. This includes helping the patient feel better about himself. Humor's use should never further the deterioration of an already depleted self-image. If it does, it is not humor.

s.
The last thing the patient needs, whose vulnerability approaches Swiss cheese, is to be denied the defense of humor. Such humor wards off feelings of inadequacy that don't need to be dwelled upon. When unrecognized and coldly penetrated, the patient experiences the humiliation of being treated like a child.

t.
Searching out the vulnerability that lies beneath humor, without sensitivity to the patient's need to strengthen himself from within, merely diminishes his sense of worth. His/her humor is a last ditch attempt to maintain the self-respect that in our own culture is an inalienable right.

u.
The negative use of humor as avoidance is more obvious (and often present) in adolescents. When a manipulative peer uses humor to exploit the fears of his fellows, he/she sets in motion what can be destructive forms of avoidance. Its naked aim is to polarize communication. It is driven by the patient's projection of con-

flicted feelings toward authority figures onto the group. It also carries a deeply rooted resentment that betrays its failure to resolve unconscious sources of aggression.

v.

Sociopathy uses humor to express hostility. Its need to overcome the feeling of being insulted has degenerated to a play for power. And its consumption of power is no longer humor by definition. Such abuse of humor is discernible by its search for a scapegoat. Sociopathy seeks a victim who can easily be belittled in the style of a bossy sibling. Its tendency is to disrupt communication. A sociopath's half-conscious aim is to intimidate the softly evolved freedom of more reticent peers. To prevent his dictatorial distortions, the sociopath should be directly confronted. This can be accomplished by honestly exploring sociopathy's emotional content, familial causes, and its impact on group members.

w.

Humor is clearly a key to my own sense of well-being. Not to mention my tennis game. When out of tune with humor I feel detached and cut off from others. At bottom, I am less loving. I am less open to the needs of others and deprive myself of personal intimacy. I enter what Roszak calls "objective consciousness" and what Buber terms an I-It relationship. I am similarly unaffected by the humorous tendency in others. My corresponding mood is "feeling depressed." As my depression subsides I am likewise more receptive to the energy humor frees. Which comes first I'm not certain. My hunch is it's a little of both. More clarity needs to be evolved as to the relationship of the two.

x.

The danger of any creative movement becoming "popular" is that its translation to the group destroys the integrity of its intent. History is replete with examples of what Ibsen calls "the crowd" reducing the noblest ideas to the banal. If we think of liberty, equality, and fraternity as ideals of "the true believer" that the herd has debased to free-market consumerism, Stalinist communism, and Hitlerian Fascism, we are at the heart of the matter. The resilient charm of humor will hopefully sustain *the common sense* of not repeating the same mistakes. Humor is an egalitarian defrocker of ideological shibboleths that can return our politics to a humanely redemptive plane.

y.

Humor is one of many ingredients in the process of healing. Its worth lies in breaking the spell of our serious self-absorption. It triggers the hope (against hope) that our obsession on guilt (including its denial) can be forgiven. Its most redeeming feature? Humor reminds us of the freedom of being human forever and ever and right now.

z-z-z.

Every day is the open door to a new beginning. But I have to sleep now in order to know what this sentence means . . . (Eight hours later) Good morning!

z-z.

Humor allows us to "forgive" (= being able to *give* in a forward-looking way that "hopes for the best") instead of positioning the pride that we assert as aggression to survive.

z.

I laugh because it's fun to laugh. And if it weren't fun, I wouldn't be laughing. I would be crying or mowing the lawn. The trick, of course, is to enjoy mowing the lawn to the point of laughing. We need to find ways to enjoy the work that we do.

SOME MORE THOUGHTS

The most I can say is humor works for me. There are, of course, countless paths to humor's actualization that escape my grasp. If we could count them we'd be in trouble. But we'd be in worse trouble if we couldn't count any.

a.

Why do we say humor "works" when what we *in reality* mean is that humor "plays"? Or is being *out of reality,* as a triumph of pleasure, the power in humor that enables humor to do what works? If our answer to either of these questions is a Socratic "I don't know," we probably understand that *how* humor plays at working in order to play, and works at playing in order to work, is the reason *why* humor exists.

e.

Hobbes was wrong when he said, "Laughter is a sudden glory arising at the sight of an inferior." Such thinking is arrogant and emotionally disturbed. It is as "sick" as his monarchial defense of absolutism in the face of democracy. Humor is at once a key to interpreting the entirety of his thought. I wonder if the same is true of every theory or "system" devoid of humor; and if humor is therefore an unexplored focus of interpretation as a method that can be critically applied.

i.

Kierkegaard was right. When given one wish by Mercury in the presence of the gods in heaven, he answered: "that I may always have the laugh on my side."[xcvii] The gods, of course, laughed.

o.

Swift was not whistling Dixie when he said to Mr. Delaney:

> "Humor is odd, grotesque, and wild,
> Only by affectations spoiled;

'Tis never by invention got;
Men have it when they know it not."[xcviii]

Nor was Alice Meynell whistling in the dark when she noted a Victorian century ago:

"The sense of humor has other things to do than to make itself conspicuous in the act of laughter."[xcix]

Consider John of Salisbury's discovery at the end of the medieval period:

"It is pleasant and not in the least unbecoming for a man of honor to indulge occasionally in reasonable mirth, but it is disgraceful to lower personal dignity by excessive indulgence in it."[c]

All three could grasp James Thurber's modern insight:

"Humor is emotional chaos remembered in tranquillity."[ci]

The sense of humor in persons so different in time and place suggests that laughter is an enduring feature of the human soul. When Twain, after all, says "There is no humor in heaven," he is speaking in the context of the secret sorrow that humor includes, and that the joy of heaven surely transcends. H. L. Mencken hits this ontic nerve on the head when he says:

"There are men so philosophical that they can see humor in their own toothaches. But there has never lived a man so philosophical that he could see the toothache in his own humor."[cii]

u.

Humor does not need laughter to exist. But it is beautiful

when they are one and the same and each is the other. What this means I am not sure, but I am sure it means something. Unless of course it means nothing. I think of Porgy and Bess: "I've got plenty of nothing and nothing's plenty for me."

CHAPTER XII

EASY FOR YOU TO LAUGH

> "Humor alone, that magnificent discovery of those who are cut short in their calling to highest endeavor, those who falling short of tragedy are as rich in gifts as in affliction, humor alone (perhaps the most inborn and brilliant achievement of the spirit) grasps the impossible and brings every aspect of human existence within the rays of its prism."
> — Herman Hesse

There is a joke about a horse who walks into a bar and the bartender asks: "Why the long face?" The art of counseling is a lot like asking this question in the guise of a punch line to a joke. Consider this observation:

> Behind the humor boom, as behind every joke, is a sad reality: Humor is one of the few tools Americans can use to mend their fraying national fabric. "There's a whole rise today of the comedian as a shaman," says Joseph Boskin, professor of history at Boston University. "Like shamans in ancient society, they understand fissures and try to heal them. In a society as diverse and conflicted as this one is, two things bring Americans together: Popular music and popular humor."[ciii]

A good comedian is a kind of modern shaman who "heals" an audience with laughter. A therapist with a sense of humor does the same thing in the first person. Because what's good for the goose is good for the gander, I'll address the healing power of humor in myself.

LAUGHTER AND FRIENDS

I don't know when I first laughed, but I recall heartily laughing at an early age with my family and friends. Friends are worth tracing by name in a conscious way. I've found remembered friends to be a revivable source of strength. My "family tree" of friends spans the journey of my life from before kindergarten to the present. All are people I've loved, and been loved by. They spark happy memories and humorous recollections. Friends form the interior of our lives and we carry them with us wherever we go. They are the barely conscious stage of everything *personal*.

Dotting this canvas of friends are vital mentors. I think fondly of Trawick. His friendship enriched and evolved my growth as a person. He was kind, generous, empathic, intellectually gifted, a student of human nature, and filled with a merry spirit. Tray was also a gifted psychiatrist and had just retired as director of GMHI in Atlanta. The youngest child of a large family, he had an astute concern for children and the underprivileged. I treasure his ways and have made some of them mine. I recall our weekly games of chess in front of the fire, and his wife, Cornelia, bringing us ice cream and shouting "Check!" Our conversations ranged from the Third World to witchcraft to education for the inmate. I have rarely felt so at home and unconditionally accepted. I accepted Tray in the same way — with care and respect. He was like a father and at the same time an equal friend. Tray's life was not without its struggles. But he always had enough time to "listen" and wisely respond. During a painful divorce, he was a rock of support.

Trawick's sudden death was a shock. In a moment of grief I felt bitter at life for being unjust, and at Trawick for leaving me in a time of need. How could he abruptly "die" without even saying good-bye? I felt guilty for having such selfish thoughts. My anger decreased as I discerned the imprint of Trawick's being on me.

This included knowing that Tray would grasp my anger as a normal stage of grief.

Humor was helpful when I remembered joking with Trawick about death. He showed no fear of death. Death was merely the other side of nature's equation whose acceptance meant living life to its fullest. Tray lived his life to the fullest in giving ways to the very end. The true context of all conflict, including its resolution, lies, I think, in coming to terms with death. Trawick helped me in more ways than he'll ever know. *

There were a few professors who left a like impression. Each was a resting place for tough questions amidst the travails of grad school. Doesn't the truth lie in asking honest questions, and not in any finite answer? Or rather, truth confirms the depth and integrity of our search. And there are mentors whose depth and integrity instill the same in ourselves. Each mentor in my case possessed a good sense of humor. Each taught me that in the face of tragedy we can still laugh. The sad side of life can be grasped in a humorous light.

I think of my divorce as a tragedy whose stage I reluctantly walked. Divorce is like the death of a friend, but harder to survive. Because the missing person is still alive, and divorce *includes rejection* by the one who knows us the best. Divorce also triggers voices of doubt and self-condemnation. What's the point? Why go on? The thought of suicide is often a comfort. Personal shortcomings grow loudly conscious. "I'm inadequate." "I'm a failure." "I'm weak." "My life can never be put back together again."

A curious theme of my Divorce Depression was the spontaneous occurrence of laughter with good friends. I found absurd relief in what was in no apparent sense laughable. I saw the flip side of laughing so hard it hurts, is hurting so bad "it laughs." There is a sublime order of laughter, beyond the tragi-comic, that puts reality in hilarious perspective in one svelte swoop. It is what the ancients called Divine Madness and Kierkegaard called "blessed" laughter. Such laughter didn't "cure" me and shedding sad tears

---
* or maybe he does know.

was important. Yet it was every bit as essential, because laughter *saw through* my despair to its resolution. In self-contained moments, I glimpsed a lucid bliss. I experienced laughter so absurdly real it shed tears of joy.

The context of such laughter was the embrace of genuine friends. I was filled with desperate feelings that only humor shared with friends could soothe. Amidst inanity, I discerned the liquidity of care that survives the absurd. Where friends are concerned love *is* blind. My friends gave my displays of wit a captive audience. They reminded me again and again that it was okay to laugh. Each time my turmoil took a humorous twist, I could see its "joke" in a fresh perspective. When alone, I returned to a dark mood, but the presence of true friends lifted my spirits immensely. Friends catalyzed a catharsis of heartfelt laughter. They did so without probing my vulnerability. They knew the truth that love *builds up*. They ignored my faults and nurtured strengths in obvious need of healing. One of those strengths was my sense of humor.

HOSTILITY AND AIKIDO

My tolerance for scab picking at this time was nil. Scab picking is the art of scratching a wound to see if it bleeds. It is what dogs do when they attack an injured member of the pack. We call it "putting salt in the wounds" that need to be healed. Scab pickers are so filled with resentment they inflict pain on others in order to quell the pain in themselves. They are more to be pitied than scorned. When feeling defenseless, however, they can do caustic harm. They are at best a last catalyst of antibodies in a slow process of healing. At worst, they deepen fresh wounds and retard healing. Blind to empathy, they are short suited in humor. They confuse humor with irony, sarcasm, and spite. We should *consider the source* of scab picking — when it comes from the likes of a jealous peer. But there are vulnerable times when we can't. I took putdowns to heart I should have countered with Aikido.

Aikido is the art of self-defense that follows the path of least resistance. Instead of meeting force with force, it is adroitly indirect. Aikido throws aggression off stride via its own momentum. My rediscovery of humor evolved a like awareness. I realized the best way to repel hostile words was with a humorous aside. What did not deserve a serious response (scab picking) could be humored. A vindictive retort could be sidestepped. It could be embraced tongue in cheek, and directly cast in a humorous light. For example: "How does it feel to be on the make?" "Not so hot, but thank you for asking."

My use of humor here was appropriately defensive. The person didn't care about my emotional condition and her remark was malicious. But why confront what would leave more quills to pick from my flesh? Especially when my courage and self-respect were at an all-time low. I didn't have the strength for a battle, no matter how small, but I could stop hostility from sapping my strength via humorous resistance.

My resistance was not cowardly or passive. It was *realistic* and in my best interest. Turning the other cheek was so ingrained in my values that I couldn't regress to the spite of an eye for an eye. But I could keep the dignity alive that humor buoys by throwing aggression off stride. Instead of incurring the wrath of an unneeded power struggle, I could "grin and bear it."

Anthropologists make much of the baring of teeth by primates as a sign of aggression. Hyenas, for example, display their teeth when threatened by an intruder. What rings as laughter in the human ear is really a mixture of hostility and fear. Death or extinction is the danger that the laughter of hyenas defends against. Anthropologists think humans do the same and are just as clannish.

Laughter *can* be a way of beating our chests. It can flaunt superiority when facing what we feel as a threat. Racist and sexist jokes are crass examples, as is the rancor in such epithets as honky, nigger, wop, chink, holly, spic, gaijin (Japanese for "foreign devil"), and guaylo (Cantonese). Such laughter is demonic and little further evolved than what animals convey with a growl. It echoes

Freud's distinction between hostile wit, harmless wit, the comic, and humor.

Freud's distinction is never clear cut, just as there are degrees of spite that can tinge the kinder laugh of humor. My *humorous resistance* may have been a way of treading water during an angry period. The complexities of modern life too often require the frank response of a growl. I sometimes growl myself while taking my shower in the morning. Growling is underrated and as important as honking at cows when driving across Nebraska. But growling brings far less pleasure than heartfelt laughter.

Nietzsche saw wisdom in terms of a camel, a lion, and a child. There is in all of us a beast of burden, the ferocity of a lion, and the joyful play of a child. Most of us, I'm afraid, have evolved no further than blind obedience. We are victims of what Nietzsche calls "the herd instinct." Do what you're told and humbly bow to whatever authority directs you in the path of certitude. We are bovine victims of a work ethic that is in no singular way Protestant. A courageous few rebel and become "individuals" in the guise of a lion's growl. We angrily show our teeth, rant and rave, and are surprised to find ourselves atop the rat race that is the survival of the fittest.

Yet only a few complete the cycle and are enough reconciled to contradictions in themselves to be reborn as a child. It is doubtful if Nietzsche reached this stage himself. He saw the possibility, however; and what made being reborn impossible for Nietzsche may (partly because of Nietzsche) make it possible for us. The archetypal hope that surrounds the Death of God is the resurrection of a "new being."

If we could understand that biogenesis is a kind of cosmic play, we could perhaps evolve beyond the baring of teeth that survival now demands. Humor, and its rootedness in play, may actually contain the ingredients of our survival. I think of the last line in Kafka's *Metamorphosis*. He writes: "And it was like a confirmation of their new dreams . . . that at the end of their journey their daughter sprang to her feet and stretched her young body."

ANOREXIA AND GANDHI

What comes to mind for some reason is death. Doesn't death relativize the trivia we take so seriously in our daily lives? We know this at a funeral in our memories of a loved one. How important is washing the car in the context of Kosovo, or when a majority of the world's children go to sleep hungry? The prosperity we tenaciously pursue shallows in comparison to our ultimate concerns. It obscures from view the fragility of life and our most decent motives. I sometimes think that anorexia is a blindly aimed ethical protest in kind. Anorexia acts out the hypocrisy of a full stomach whose conclusion in search of meaning is self-denial. Confronting the same loss of purpose as Kafka's *hunger artist*, the anorexic (most of whom are female), literally starves herself to death.

Anorexia's epidemic proportions suggest social causes beyond familial quirks, or a fear of pubescence in the image of a Barbie doll. Its contortions mask a desperate need to be "real" amidst the banality of material comforts. We worship gadgets, money, work, and expendable "stuff" at the cost of commitment. The first hint of a failure in "the other" to meet immediate needs, triggers flight from a recognition of the emptiness in ourselves.

Our values are crassly commercial. We treat each other as discarded commodities when no longer of use. To embellish the virtues of a serious condition, anorexia is at least honest. It mirrors the emaciated interior of our lives and a "death wish" society as a whole denies. Namely, our pragmatic fixation on treating people as things. It confronts the utility of changing partners instead of patterns.

Am I off base to think anorexia is unconsciously linked to the same critique of society that informed the likes of a Gandhi, a King, or a Mother Theresa? Lacking vision, however, anorexia reverts to a narcissism that is sacrificial. Whatever the answer, anorexia and the repression of its causes are too rigidly serious. Neither partakes of the anecdote to life's sobriety in relation to death that humor provides. As A. A. Cooper puts it: "Humor is the only test of gravity; and gravity of humor. For a subject that does not bear raillery is suspicious; and a jest that does not bear a serious examination is certainly false wit." Enter humor stage right.

VENTING THE SPLEEN

Humor is never tightly bound like a bowel in need of an enema. It flows freely without constriction and in playful disregard of *ought* or *should*. The metaphor is worth pursuing because of humor's movement beyond what Freud terms anal retentive and anal expulsive. Take slang expressions like "tight assed" and "getting your shit together." They bodily express Freud's search for a balance between both extremes. The word *diabolical* is similarly suggestive via its literal roots of *mud* and *to sling*. Because humor is fluid, and as it were moves, it resists slinging mud *à la* venting our spleens. Humor's playful intent is well beyond the excretion of repressed aggression. At the same time humor avoids spreading chaos like Chicken Little. Instead, humor is "constructive" and relativizes *everything particular* within a unity of movement. Humor relaxes in the wisdom of Kierkegaard that "the best cure for a cramp in the foot is to step on it."

HUMOR AND PLAY

To have been loved as a child clearly opens us to humor as adults. Sensing humor in the present includes every humorous experience in the past. Every time we laugh we revive the feelings of laughter (like the sense of scent) through childhood to the womb. I was lucky to have had a mother who loved me like a rock. She had a good sense of humor, and my dad's sense of humor was delightful. I remember laughing with gusto and feeling tickled in the whole of my being. I also recall quietly chuckling. And before that, intuitively, feeling amused by nature and the flowers, butterflies, birds, and bees. I remember my fascination in a sandbox at an ant crawling across my feet.

We are bonded to nature in a funny way that is essentially simple. What I imagine, but cannot prove, is *a pool of joy* (we after all assume a "pain pool") that moistens humor from below. I catch glimpses of a hidden shelf of *humours* that mix the particularities of a laugh. The abundance of joker and trickster figures in the folklore of primitive cultures suggests such a source (Cf., Radin's *The Trickster*). Humor's primal source seems deeper even than language. Humor is an archetypal fluid of the senses whose imagination is genetically transmitted.

Homo sapiens, of course, has no monopoly on humor. Chimpanzees, for example, are less than serious, and 98% of our genes are the same. Their playful traits suggest play's evolution through the animal kingdom. The projection of play onto fellow creatures is more than anthropomorphic. A Stanford anthropologist, for example, claims impish pranks to be a trait of the gorillas she has reared to adulthood. My only verification of this was a college roommate who acted like a gorilla. I have no doubt, however, that kittens, cubs, and puppies do frolic. I know this because I've frolicked with my cocker spaniel. I wish we could map the creaturely evolution of play. But that may be by definition what play is not.

I confuse the difference between humor and play because their difference is confusing. Their subjective bond is too mutual to distinguish. Play is broader and is *the context* of humor as a mood. Thus all humor is playful, but all play is not necessarily humorous. Sexuality, for example, is at root playful. It requires trust and a dropping of pretense to the point of accepting and responding to the playfulness of the other. And humor can heighten such play, even to ecstasy.

Humor and play occur at varying levels of intensity and enhance the grasp and actualization of each other. Both coax a trust whose fulfillment they mutually enjoy. Play and humor share the free feeling of losing ourselves in the moment. They combine concentration and relaxation and "letting go" of conscious control.

There are as many styles of therapy as there are therapists, and this includes therapy for ourselves. I know that humor works for me (as do tennis, clarity, faith, Scrabble, acceptance, etc.). By the same token, there are as many paths as there are people seeking a healthy frame of mind. My hope is that what works for me will work for others.

My hunch is there are a lot of people in whom humor triggers healing. Diehard opponents of humor bother me at this point, especially when they're clinicians. Such people are rigid, impacted, and too sure of their views to be trusted. Self-doubt is not only a precondition of the truth; it is the midwife of truth's perception. Likewise, humor is the truest test of gravity.

MOTHER EARTH

Humor's secret may be as simple as facing what we are. Spiritually, and biologically, we are the breathing embodiment of Mother Earth. In accord with Goethe's legend, we are living clay, formed by and in the hands of Care. Care is present at birth and weans the curl of our first smile. It guides the imagination. Our hopes and dreams, and how we care, are ways of *humoring* reality. Care is at the heart of what renders anxiety sweet. Its role is as basic as the poster on an old professor's door. The poster shows the blue earth as seen from outer space. The caption says: LOVE YOUR MOTHER. Our blue dot of life amid billions of stars is our "home" and original mother.

The last laugh belongs to those among us who are as rich in gifts as in affliction. Bill Cosby, Art Buchwald, and Gilda Radner are remarkable examples. Each in their way saw humor as a gift, and knew it was more blessed to give than receive.

After the tragic loss of his son, Bill Cosby says without rancor: "Ennis was my hero." More than anyone I can think of, as a professional comedian, Cosby has put his money where his mouth is. To conquer his grief, he's been doing comedy across the country for charitable causes. He's managed to keep his sense of humor intact by bringing laughter to others. Cosby continues to remind us: "If you can laugh at it, you can survive it." What a role model Bill Cosby has been.

Buchwald's mother was schizophrenic and he was dumped in an orphanage at an early age. He's battled suicide, suffered two clinical depressions, and considers laughter the key to his survival.[civ] Gilda Radner, in her autobiography, similarly calls cancer: "The most unfunny thing there is." She faced death as she faced life — as a comedian. She never gave up. Her posthumous book is a way of asking: Why the long face?

CHAPTER XIII

APPENDIX AND LIVER

> The survival of civilization depends to a significant degree upon our capacity for humor. People who laugh together are less inclined to kill one another.
> — Conrad Lorenz (*On Aggression*)

Groucho Marx told an amusing joke that applies to our subject. A man at wit's end has taken his cousin to a psychiatrist, "Doc, you gotta help me!" he says. "What's the problem?" asks the psychiatrist. "It's my cousin. He thinks he's a chicken. "A what?!" "A chicken. He thinks he's a chicken." "How long has this been going on?" "For about five years now." "Five years! Well, why didn't you bring him in before now?" The man answers, "We needed the eggs."

There lies the relevance of humor to therapy. We need the eggs. Considering the chickens who lay our eggs, the "funny farm" is aptly named. For humor is an abnormal elixir for an abnormal condition. As B. C. Lane puts it:

> "Many of us would love to experience a political and personal reality different from what we know, but we're afraid others might think us soft-headed, foolish, even mad. We need the Holy Fool and prophetic storyteller among us — the one who lives by a different reality, deliberately breaking down the structures seen as most sacred and traditional by others."[cv]

Humor's need *to be* is relief from the anxiety our seriousness compulsively hides. We are the consummate realists. We look askance at nonsense because it can't be measured in dollars and cents. We short circuit humor for the sake of cutthroat standards of success. Simply, we take ourselves too seriously. We are like the spoiled child who always gets his way. We are retentively practical toward whatever fails to yield an expedient result.

Who can deny our results? We are unmatched experts at filtering pieces of matter through the grid of spatial analysis. There seems to be no object, no matter how remote, that lies beyond our rational grasp. But we are more nearsighted than Mr. Magoo when it come to penetrating the heart of the human condition. Does not our obsession with conquering outer space belie a paralysis of the space within?

We *are* the hollow men. Loin-clothed pygmies better understand the inner reverie of play. They curiously roll over on their backs when they laugh. We, in contrast, struggle to maintain our composure. We identify the same as being civilized. What "civilization" represses includes our sense of humor. As Freud puts it:

> "The power of reason usually grows so strong during the latter part of childhood and during the period of education which extends over the age of puberty, that the pleasure in freed nonsense rarely dares manifest itself. One fears to utter nonsense."[cvi]

The Muppet Show notwithstanding, Freud's analysis still applies. Too many of us are afraid "to utter nonsense." When humor is presented to us by another, we quickly prick the vulnerability it reveals. Our disaffection betrays the need to punish what has been punished in ourselves. We spank the proverbial bottom of play because of the same rejection of the child in ourselves. We thus reenact the childhood rite of impatient force throttling "freed nonsense." In spurning the kinship of humor, we blame "the other" for the void of affection in ourselves.

The kinder intent of humor is affirmation. Humor gently confronts the resentment that drives our compulsion to overachieve. What humor revives is the formative juices of self-acceptance. It softens the seriousness of our condition in the light of kindness. To demean this most human of impulses is to demean what is most human in ourselves. We choose neither to care nor to be cared for. There lies my distrust of intellectualizing.

Indeed, many intellectuals are as emotionally in tune with humor as a kangaroo in heat. The majority of our administrators and power-grabbing executives are even worse. They fail to grasp the obvious, most crucial ingredient of intelligence. Namely, the feeling that gives rise to every concept and linguistic form in the first place. I question the intelligence of anyone who places rational cognition above emotional sensitivity. The best he can do is perpetuate alienation in those who follow his example, without regard for what's decent and human. And how intelligent is that? The basis of everything intellectual is a mixture of moral forces and the projection of what we feel. Anyone who misses this truth is likely blind to humor. He/she forgets that to be wise is not to be afraid to be kind.

Woody Allen makes the point that "Until we have a resolution to our terror, we're going to have an expedient culture."[cvii] I agree in part. Expediency is a reaction against the legacy of grandiose thinking (e.g., German Idealism expanded to the collapsed arrogance of Adolf Hitler) inherited from the last century. What humor cuts short is mental masturbation in the style of Herr Professor. I have nothing against masturbation, and am merely making a point. Spinning the wool of abstraction, however, can be very dangerous. When coupled with patriotism, as it was in Germany, it can lead to elitism, absolutism, and Fascism. Just as speculative psychology without a practical instinct misses the point of therapy.

The well-intended aim of expedience is to counter this tendency. Yet clearly the expediency of our culture contributes in part to our terror. Whether the chicken or egg came first, the egg still produces a chicken. I have written this book in hopes of countering both extremes. My hope is that humorous insemination can evolve a swan. What I'm asking, I guess, is, why a chicken?

Humor stands as a natural corrective to both extremes. It clearly doesn't fit our "efficiency to the nth degree" scheme of things.* The relief humor provides instead coincides with a dropping of cognitive pretense. It thus amounts to a relaxation of conscious control over our presently repressed search for transcendence. To transcend means to go beyond the normal boundaries of awareness. Enter the *foolish* proximity of humor to the likes of feeling, paradox, and ultimate concern. Our fear of the latter is the deeper cause of humor's repression. We are afraid of the existential questions humor prompts us to ask. Who am I in relation to God, the universe, my fellow beings?

The beauty of humor is that it rises above the gravity of such questions. It enjoys the moment and knows that writing about "the laughter factor" is a far cry from feeling its presence. Just as analyzing the mechanics of sex is a quantum leap from making love to one's beloved. In the immortal words of E. B. White: "Humor can be dissected as a frog can, but the thing dies in the process and the innards are discouraging to any but the pure scientific mind."[cviii] Hopefully, this essay has not prompted the death of humor. My intent has been the opposite, and to remind you to laugh.

As for myself, I generally laugh in spurts of three. Or ha, ha, ha. These spurts are unpredictable, come from within, and are especially fun when shared with others. They have been a recurring source of pleasure, and triggered reverberations of hope in the depths of my soul. They have brought joy, compassion, and a heartfelt sense of contentment. I have experienced in their presence the uncanny assurance that there is more to the universe than black holes, barbarism, and bronchitis. My spurts of laughter are what prompted me to write this book. I hope you are more in touch with the laughter in yourself as a result.

---

* I just opened a Chinese fortune cookie. It says, "He who hurries cannot walk with dignity."

ENDNOTES

Chapter I

i   *Dictionary of American Maxims*, edited by David Kin (New York: Philosophical Library, Inc., MCMLV), p. 244.

ii *Dictionary of Quotations*, edited by Bergan Evans, p. 331.

iii Op. Cit., *Dictionary of American Maxims*, p. 244.

Chapter II

iv Antony Chapman and Hugh Foot, ed., *It's a Funny Thing, Humor* (Oxford: Pergamon Press, 1977), p. 27.

Chapter III

v   James Wandersee, *The American Biology Teacher*, Volume 44, #44, April, 1982.

vi L. Berk, "Neuroendocrine and Stress Hormone Changes During Mirthful Laughter," *American Journal of Medical Sciences*. 1989; 298: 390-396.

vii L. Berk, Interview with J. R. Dunn. *Humor and Health Letter*, 1994; 3(6): 1-8.

viii K. Dillon, "Positive Emotional States and Enhancement of the Immune System." *International J Psychiatry in Medicine*, 1985. 5(1).

Chapter IV

ix Sigmund Freud, *Wit and Its Relation to the Unconscious*, from Brill's translation of *The Basic Writings of Sigmund Freud* New York: Random House, 1938) p. 708.

Chapter V

x   Ibid.

xi Sigmund Freud, *Character and Culture* (New York: Macmillan Publishing Co., 1963), p. 268.

xii Norman O. Brown, *Life Against Death* (Middleton, Connecticut: Wesleyan University Press, 1959), p. 62.

xiii	Op. Cit., Freud, *Wit and Its Relation to the Unconscious*, p. 719.
xiv	Ibid.
xv	Op. Cit., Freud, *Character and Culture*, p. 268.
xvi	Op. Cit., Chapman, p. 157.
xvii	Ibid., p. 158.
xviii	Op. Cit., Chapman, p. 157.

Chapter VI

xix	Op. Cit., Huizinga, *Homo Ludens* (Boston: Beacon Press, 1950), p. 158.

Chapter VII

xx	Soren Kierkegaard, *Journals and Papers*, edited by Hong and Hong Bloomington: Indiana University Press, 1970), Volume I, p. 260.
xxi	Ibid., Volume II, p. 255.
xxii	Chris Rock, *Rock This*, Chris Rock Enterprises, Inc., New York: 1997, p. 17.
xxiii	Belden C. Lane, "The Spirituality and Politics of Holy Folly," *The Christian Century*, December 15, 1982.

Chapter VIII

xxiv	*Parables of Kierkegaard*, edited by Thomas C. Oden (Princeton: Princeton University Press, 1978), p. 3.
xxv	Ibid., p. 19.
xxvi	Ibid., p. 20.
xxvii	Ibid., p. 125.

Chapter IX

xxviii	Op. Cit., Freud, *Wit and Its Relation to the Unconscious*, p. 633.
xxix	Ibid., p. 638.
xxx	Ibid., P. 633.
xxxi	Ibid., P. 658.
xxxii	Ibid., p. 657.
xxxiii	Ibid., p. 639.
xxxiv	Ibid., p. 644.

xxxv Ibid., p. 647.
xxxvi Ibid., p. 649.
xxxvii Ibid., p. 650.
xxxviii Ibid., p. 650-651.
xxxix Ibid., p. 653.
xl Ibid., p. 655-656.
xli Ibid., p. 656.
xlii Ibid., p. 658.
xliii Ibid., p. 657.
xliv Ibid., p. 633.
xlv Ibid., p. 664.
xlvi Ibid., p. 667.
xlvii Ibid., p. 669.
xlviii Ibid., p. 670.
xlix Ibid., p. 673.
l Ibid., p. 674.
li Ibid., p. 676.
lii Ibid., p. 679.
liii Ibid., p. 681.
liv Ibid., p. 682.
lv Ibid., p. 684.
lvi Ibid., p. 697.
lvii Ibid., p. 698.
lviii Ibid., p. 698.
lix Ibid., p. 702.
lx Ibid., p. 710.
lxi Ibid., p. 711.
lxii Ibid., p. 712.
lxiii Ibid., p. 714.
lxiv Ibid., p. 717.
lxv Ibid., p. 719.
lxvi Ibid., p. 719.
lxvii Ibid., p. 720.
lxviii Ibid., p. 723.
lxix Ibid., p. 718.

lxx	Ibid., p. 717.
lxxi	Ibid., p. 718.
lxxii	Ibid., p. 721.
lxxiii	Ibid., p. 722.
lxxiv	Ibid., p. 717.
lxxv	Ibid., p. 730.
lxxvi	Ibid., p. 731.
lxxvii	Ibid., p. 735.
lxxviii	Ibid., p. 734.
lxxix	Ibid., p. 740.
lxxx	Ibid., p. 803.
lxxxi	Ibid., p. 797.
lxxxii	Ibid., p. 798.
lxxxiii	Ibid., p. 802.
lxxxiv	Ibid., p. 802.
lxxxv	Bruno Bettelheim, "Freud and the Soul," *The New Yorker*, March, 1982.

Chapter X

lxxxvi	Soren Kierkegaard, *Journals and Papers*, edited by Hong and Hong (Bloomington: Indiana University Press, 1970), Volume I, p. 255.
lxxxvii	Ibid., Volume III, p. 151.
lxxxviii	Conrad Hyers, *Holy Laughter* (Philadelphia Westminster Press, 1972), p. 22.
lxxxix	Op. Cit., Freud, *Character and Culture*, p. 269.
xc	Op. Cit., Hyers, pp. 27-28.
xci	Op. Cit., Kierkegaard, *Journals and Papers*, Volume I, p. 444.
xcii	Ibid., p. 444.
xciii	Friedrich Nietzsche, *Thus Spoke Zarathustra*, Walter Kaufmann's translation in *The Portable Nietzsche* (New York: Viking Press, 1954), p. 408.
xciv	Ibid., p. 405.

Chapter XI

xcv	Op. Cit., Conrad Hyers, *The Comic Vision and the Christian Faith*, p. 31.
xcvi	Op. Cit., Freud, *Character and Culture*, p. 269.
xcvii	Soren Kierkegaard, *The Laughter is on My Side*, ed. by Poole and Stangerup (Princeton, Princeton University Press, 1989), p. 241.

xcviii	Johnathan Swift: *To Mr. Delaney*
xcix	Alice Meynell: *Laughter* (19th century).
c	John of Salisbury: *Policraticus*, I, 8, 48. (12th century).
ci	James Thurber, as quoted in The New York Post, Feb 29, 1960.
cii	H.L. Mencken, *Chrestomathy*, 618.

Chapter XII

ciii	Cynthia Crossen, *The Wall Street Journal* (January 31, 1997), p. A-12.
civ	Art Buchwald, *Leaving Home*, Ballantine Books, New York: 1994, p. 79.

Chapter XIII

cv	Beldon C. Lane, "The Spirituality and Politics of Holy Folly," *The Christian Century*, December 15, 1982, p. 1281.
cvi	Op. Cit., Freud, *Wit and Its Relation to the Unconscious*, p. 634.
cvii	Jack Kroll, "Woody," *Newsweek*, April 24, 1978.
cviii	Op. Cit., Chapman, p. 127.

EPILOGUE

One of the most interesting things about humor as therapy is so little has been written about it. Most therapists I know accept various forms of humor and play as critical to the process of psychological healing. Norman Cousins and others have underscored the importance of those elements in physical healing as well. But the professional community still isn't giving humor the attention it deserves; and I am gratified to see a book of the caliber Dan Keller has written, a book dedicated to the role of humor in psychotherapy. He has kept the integrity of both strategy and the subtle relationship of humor to psychotherapy intact.

We must acknowledge that a tremendous number of variables inform the humorous encounter. Can we as therapists learn to structure such complicated patterns and even reproduce them? Can we at least learn (and teach our students) to recognize and affirm such events when they occur spontaneously? Knowledge of the work of, say, Milton H. Erickson suggests that some therapists can and do operate consciously on this level. It is my strong belief that most, if not all, effective therapists do so unconsciously. I'm certain that is true for me. I cannot separate humor and therapy, just as I cannot separate paradox and therapy. One is the other. A great many colleagues from various schools of therapy have essentially told me the same thing. "If my humor left me I would be no good for my patients, and no good to myself. They would stay crazy and I would go crazy."

If humor is so important to therapists, then where do we go to learn to be humorous? It's ironic. There are literally hundreds of books that will help you learn dream analysis and hundreds more that will teach you paraphrase. But how many books, or graduate courses, or seminars are there to teach therapists humor? About three. More coming, I think, but very few at the present time. Which brings us back to this book. For most readers, I believe its value will be in the stories it tells. Dan Keller has filled his pages with countless anecdotes from his own practice, describing the application of various kinds of humor tactics with various kinds of clients. He has added dozens more from his personal life. Reading Dan's stories, I began to speculate how similar tactics, strategies and humorous twists might be applied in my own work. I hope his book does the same for you.

Toward the end of his book, Dr. Keller notes, "Diehard opponents of humor bother me at this point ... They feel rigid, impacted, and oddly constipated." The word "pathetic" comes to mind as well. It's like being opposed to light. If you don't want to see green badly enough, you can close your eyes. But the electromagnetic radiation that surrounds you isn't going to go away. Its utility won't be lost to anyone but you. If you continue to avoid it, you are going to have to keep your eyes closed (or do something even more drastic). And sooner or later you are going to be run over by a bus.

Psychotherapy provides endless examples of, and opportunities to employ humor, in all its forms and guises. Whether or not you choose to take advantage of them is up to you. If you do, Dan Keller's book will help you. If you don't, I think you're missing a bet.

Gerald W. Piaget, Ph.D.
Portola Valley, California